Silent Dancing:
A Partial Remembrance
of a Puerto Rican Childhood

Judith Ortiz Cofer

Arte Publico Press
Houston
Texas
1990

This book is made possible by a grant from the National Endowment for the Arts, a federal agency.

Grateful acknowledgment is made to the editors of the publications in which the following essays first appeared: "Casa," *Prairie Schooner*, (Reprinted from *Prairie Schooner*, by permission of University of Nebraska Press. Copyright 1989 by University of Nebraska Press); "More Room" and "Talking to the Dead," *Puerto del Sol*; "Primary Lessons," *Great Stream Review*, and "Silent Dancing," in *The Georgia Review*.

The following poems were originally published in *Terms of Survival*, Arte Público Press, 1987; "El Olvido," "San Antonio al Revés," "Holly" and "Common Ground." Copyright 1987 by Judith Ortiz Cofer. "The Woman Who Was Left at the Altar," "Claims," "House Painter," "Schoolyard Magic," "The Way My Mother Walked," "My Father in the Navy," "En Mis Ojos No Hay Días," and "The Habit of Movement" were published in *Reaching for the Mainland*, as part of the trilogy, *Triple Crown*, copyright 1987 by the Bilingual Press/Editorial Bilingüe (Arizona State University, Tempe, AZ). Reprinted by permission of the Bilingual Press/Editorial Bilingüe.

"Lessons of the Past" first appeared in *The Georgia Review*, "Christmas, 1961" *Great Stream Review*, "Fulana" in *The Americas Review*.

Versions of the folktale, "María Sabida," and other Puerto Rican/Spanish folk wisdom were adapted from *Folklore Portorriqueño*, a collection edited by Rafael Ramírez de Arellano and published in Madrid in 1926.

The author wishes to thank several colleagues and friends for reading the essays and sharing their skills and expertise as the essays were being composed: Betty Jean Craige of the University of Georgia, and Mary Alice Morgan at Macon College, in particular, as well as others who answered my questions and listened to my stories. I want to credit Hilma Wolitzer for first suggesting that I write my family *cuentos* as personal essays after a poetry reading I did at the Bread Loaf Writers' Conference in 1987.

Work on this book was made possible by a grant from the Witter Bynner Foundation for Poetry in 1988. The essays were begun and completed during two residencies at the Hambidge Center for Creative Arts and Sciences in 1987 and 1989.

The author also wishes to acknowledge the National Endowment for the Arts for a Fellowship in Poetry awarded to her in 1989.

Ortiz Cofer, Judith, 1952–
    Silent dancing: a partial remembrance of a Puerto Rican childhood / Judith Ortiz Cofer.
    p.   cm.
    ISBN 1-55885-015-5 (alk. paper)
    1. Biography—Youth. 2. Authors, American—20th century—Biography—Youth. 3. Puerto Rico—Social life and customs. I. Title.
PS3565.R7737Z477 1990
818'.5403–dc20   89-77428
[B]   CIP

A woman writing thinks back through her mothers.

—Virginia Woolf, *A Room of One's Own*

This book is dedicated to my mother, Fanny Morot Ortiz, and to my daughter, Tanya Cofer.

Contents

Silent Dancing

Preface:
Journey to a Summer's Afternoon

As one gets older, childhood years are often conveniently consolidated into one perfect summer's afternoon. The events can be projected on a light blue screen; the hurtful parts can be edited out, and the moments of joy brought in sharp focus to the foreground. It is our show. But with all that on the cutting room floor, what remains to tell?

Virginia Woolf, whose vision guided my efforts as I tried to recall the faces and words of the people who are a part of my "summer's afternoon," wrote of the problem of writing truth from memory. In "A Sketch of the Past" she says, "But if I turn to my mother, how difficult it is to single her out as she really was; to imagine what she was thinking, to put a single sentence into her mouth." She accepts the fact that in writing about one's life, one often has to rely on that combination of memory, imagination, and strong emotion that may result in "poetic truth." In preparing to write her memoirs Woolf said, "I dream, I make up pictures of a summer's afternoon."

In one of her essays from her memoir *Moments of Being*, Woolf recalls the figure of her beautiful and beloved mother who died while the author was still a child, leaving her a few precious "moments of being" from which the mature woman must piece together a childhood. And she does so not to showcase her life, extraordinary as it was, but rather out of a need most of us feel at some point to study ourselves and our lives in retrospect; to understand what people and events formed us (and, yes, what and who hurt us, too).

From "A Sketch of the Past": "Many bright colours;

11

many distinct sounds; some human beings, caricatures; several violent moments of being, always including a circle of the scene they cut out: and all surrounded by a vast space—that is a rough visual description of childhood. This is how I shape it; and how I see myself as a child ... "

This passage illustrates the approach that I was seeking in writing about my family. I wanted the essays to be, not just family history, but also creative explorations of known territory. I wanted to trace back through scenes based on my "moments of being" the origins of my creative imagination. As a writer, I am, like most artists, interested in the genesis of ideas: How does a poem begin? Can the process be triggered at will? What compells some of us to examine and re-examine our lives in poems, stories, novels, memoirs?

Much of my writing begins as a meditation on past events. But memory for me is the "jumping off" point; I am not, in my poetry and my fiction writing, a slave to memory. I like to believe that the poem or story contains the "truth" of art rather than the factual, historical truth that the journalist, sociologist, scientist— most of the rest of the world—must adhere to. Art gives me that freedom. But in writing these "essays" (the Spanish word for essay, *ensayo*, suits my meaning here better—it can mean "a rehearsal," an exercise or practice), I faced the possibility that the past is mainly a creation of the imagination also, although there are facts one can research and confirm. The biographer's time-honored task can be employed on one's own life too. There are birth, marriage, and death certificates on file, there are letters and family photographs in someone's desk or attic; and there are the relatives who have assigned themselves the role of genealogist or family bard, recounting at the least instigation the entire history of your clan. One can go to these sources and come up with a *Life* in several volumes that will make your mother proud and give you the satisfaction of having "preserved" something. I am not interested in merely "canning" memories, however, and Woolf gave me the focus that I needed to justify this work. Its intention is not to chronicle my life—which in my case is still very much "in-progress," nor are there any extraordinary accomplishments to showcase; neither is it meant to be a record of public events and personal histories (in fact, since most of the characters in these essays are based on actual, living persons and real places, whenever I felt that it was necessary to protect their identities, I changed names, locations, etc.). Then, what is the purpose of calling this collection non-fiction or a memoir? Why not just call it fiction? Once again I must turn to my literary mentor for this project, Virginia Woolf, for an answer: like her, I wanted to try to connect myself to the threads of lives that have touched mine and at some point converged into the tapestry that is my memory of childhood. Virginia Woolf understood that the very act of reclaiming her memories could provide a writer with confidence in the power of art to discover meaning and truth in ordinary events. She was a time-traveler who saw the past as a real place one could return to by following the tracks left by strong emotions: "I feel that strong emotion must leave its trace; and it is only a question of discovering how we can get ourselves attached to it, so that we shall be able to live our lives through from the start."[1]

It was this winding path of memory, marked by strong emotions that I followed in my *ensayos* of a life.

---

[1] All quotes by Virginia Woolf are from *Moments of Being*, (Harcourt Brace Jovanovich, Inc.).

Casa

At three or four o'clock in the afternoon, the hour of *café con leche*, the women of my family gathered in Mamá's living room to speak of important things and to tell stories for the hundredth time, as if to each other, meant to be overheard by us young girls, their daughters. In Mamá's house (everyone called my grandmother Mamá) was a large parlor built by my grandfather to his wife's exact specifications so that it was always cool, facing away from the sun. The doorway was on the side of the house so no one could walk directly into her living room. First they had to take a little stroll through and around her beautiful garden where prize-winning orchids grew in the trunk of an ancient tree she had hollowed out for that purpose. This room was furnished with several mahogany rocking chairs, acquired at the births of her children, and one intricately carved rocker that had passed down to Mamá at the death of her own mother. It was on these rockers that my mother, her sisters and my grandmother sat on these afternoons of my childhood to tell their stories, teaching each other and my cousin and me what it was like to be a woman, more specifically, a Puerto Rican woman. They talked about life on the island, and life in *Los Nueva Yores*, their way of referring to the U.S., from New York City to California: the other place, not home, all the same. They told real-life stories, though

14

as I later learned, always embellishing them with a little or a lot of dramatic detail, and they told *cuentos*, the morality and cautionary tales told by the women in our family for generations: stories that became a part of my subconscious as I grew up in two worlds, the tropical island and the cold city, and which would later surface in my dreams and in my poetry.

One of these tales was about the woman who was left at the altar. Mamá liked to tell that one with histrionic intensity. I remember the rise and fall of her voice, the sighs, and her constantly gesturing hands, like two birds swooping through her words. This particular story would usually come up in a conversation as a result of someone mentioning a forthcoming engagement or wedding. The first time I remember hearing it, I was sitting on the floor at Mamá's feet, pretending to read a comic book. I may have been eleven or twelve years old: at that difficult age when a girl is no longer a child who can be ordered to leave the room if the women wanted freedom to take their talk into forbidden zones, or really old enough to be considered a part of their conclave. I could only sit quietly, pretending to be in another world, while absorbing it all in a sort of unspoken agreement of my status as silent auditor. On this day, Mamá had taken my long, tangled mane of hair into her ever busy hands. Without looking down at me or interrupting her flow of words, she began braiding my hair, working at it with the quickness and determination which characterized all her actions. My mother was watching us impassively from her rocker across the room. On her lips played a little ironic smile. I would never sit still for *her* ministrations, but even then, I instinctively knew that she did not possess Mamá's matriarchal power to command and keep everyone's attention. This was particularly evident in the spell she cast when telling a story.

"It is not like it used to be when I was a girl." Mamá announced, "Then, a man could leave a girl standing at the church altar with a bouquet of fresh flowers in her hands and disappear off the face of the earth. No way to track him down if he was from another town. He could be a married man, with maybe even two or three families all over the island. There was no way to know. And there were men who did this. Hombres with the devil in their flesh who would come to a pueblo, like this one, take a job at one of the haciendas, never meaning to stay, only to have a good time and to seduce the women."

The whole time she was speaking, Mamá was weaving my hair into a flat plait which required pulling apart the two sections of hair with little jerks that made my eyes water; but knowing how grandmother detested whining and *boba* (sissy) tears, as she called them, I just sat up as straight and stiff as I did at La Escuela San José, where the nuns enforced good posture with a flexible plastic ruler they bounced off slumped shoulders and heads. As Mamá's story progressed, I noticed how my young aunt Laura had lowered her eyes, refusing to meet Mamá's meaningful gaze. Laura was seventeen, in her last year of high school, and already engaged to a boy from another town who had staked his claim with a tiny diamond ring, then left for Los Nueva Yores to make his fortune. They were planning to get married in a year; but Mamá had expressed serious doubts that the wedding would ever take place. In Mamá's eyes, a man set free without a legal contract was a man lost. She believed that marriage was not something men desired, but simply the price they had to pay for the privilege of children, and of course, for what no decent (synonymous with "smart") woman would give away for free.

"María la Loca was only seventeen when *it* happened to her." I listened closely at the mention of this name. María was a town "character," a fat middle-aged woman who lived with her old mother on the outskirts of town. She was to be seen around the pueblo delivering the meat pies the two women made for a living. The most peculiar thing about María, in my eyes, was that she walked and moved like a little girl, though she had the thick body and wrinkled face of an old woman. She would swing her hips in an exaggerated, clownish way, and sometimes even hop and skip up to someone's house. She spoke to no one. Even if you asked her a question, she would just look at you and smile, showing her yellow teeth. But I had heard that if you got close enough, you could hear her humming a tune without words. The kids yelled out nasty things at her, calling her *la Loca*, and the men who hung out at the bodega playing dominoes sometimes whistled mockingly as she passed by with her funny, outlandish walk. But María seemed impervious to it all, carrying her basket of *pasteles* like a grotesque Little Red Riding Hood through the forest.

María la Loca interested me, as did all the eccentrics and "crazies" of our pueblo. Their weirdness was a measuring stick I used in my serious quest for a definition of "normal." As a Navy brat, shuttling between New Jersey and the pueblo, I was constantly made to feel like an oddball by my peers, who made fun of my two-way accent: a Spanish accent when I spoke English; and, when I spoke Spanish, I was told that I sounded like a "Gringa." Being the outsiders had already turned my brother and me into cultural chameleons, developing early the ability to blend into a crowd, to sit and read quietly in a fifth story apartment building for days and days when it was too bitterly cold to play outside;

or, set free, to run wild in Mamá's realm, where she took charge of our lives, releasing mother for a while from the intense fear for our safety that our father's absences instilled in her. In order to keep us from harm when father was away, mother kept us under strict surveillance. She even walked us to and from Public School No. 11, which we attended during the months we lived in Paterson, New Jersey, our home base in the States. Mamá freed the three of us like pigeons from a cage. I saw her as my liberator and my model. Her stories were parables from which to glean the *Truth*.

"María la Loca was once a beautiful girl. Everyone thought she would marry the Méndez boy." As everyone knew, Rogelio Méndez was no other than the richest man in town. "But," Mamá continued, knitting my hair with the same intensity she was putting into her story," this *macho* made a fool out of her and ruined her life." She paused for the effect of her use of the word "macho," which at that time had not yet become a popular epithet for an unliberated man. This word had for us the crude and comical connotation of "male of the species," stud; a *macho* was what you put in a pen to increase your stock.

I peeked over my comic book at my mother. She too was under Mamá's spell, smiling conspiratorially at this little swipe at men. She was safe from Mamá's contempt in this area. Married at an early age, an unspotted lamb, she had been accepted by a good family of strict Spaniards whose name was old and respected, though their fortune had been lost long before my birth. In a rocker Papá had painted sky blue sat Mamá's oldest child, Aunt Nena. Mother of three children, stepmother of two more, she was a quiet woman who liked books but had married an ignorant and abusive widower whose main interest in life was accumulating wealth. He too was in the mainland working on his dream of returning home rich and triumphant to buy the *finca* of his dreams. She was waiting for him to send for her. She would leave her children with Mamá for several years while the two of them slaved away in factories. He would one day be a rich man, and she a sadder woman. Even now her life-light was dimming. She spoke little, an aberration in Mamá's house, and she read avidly, as if storing up spiritual food for the long winters that awaited her in Los Nueva Yores without her family. But even Aunt Nena came alive to Mamá's words, rocking gently, her hands over a thick book in her lap. Her daughter, my cousin Sara, played jacks by herself on the tile porch outside the room where we sat. She was a year older than I. We shared a bed and all our family's secrets. Collaborators in search of answers, Sara and I discussed everything we heard the women say, trying to fit it all together like a puzzle that once assembled would reveal life's mysteries to us. Though she and I still enjoyed taking part in boy's games—chase, volleyball and even *vaqueros*, the island version of cowboys and Indians involving cap-gun battles and violent shootouts under the mango tree in Mamá's backyard— we loved best the quiet hours in the afternoon when the men were still at work and the boys had gone to play serious baseball at the park. Then Mamá's house belonged only to us women. The aroma of coffee perking in the kitchen, the mesmerizing creaks and groans of the rockers, and the women telling their lives in *cuentos* are forever woven into the fabric of my imagination, braided like my hair that day I felt my grandmother's hands teaching me about strength, her voice convincing me of the power of story-telling.

That day Mamá told of how the beautiful María had fallen prey to a man whose name was never the same

in subsequent versions of the story; it was Juan one
time, José, Rafael, Diego, another. We understood that
the name, and really any of the facts, were not important, only that a woman had allowed love to defeat her.
Mamá put each of us in María's place by describing her
wedding dress in loving detail: how she looked like a
princess in her lace as she waited at the altar. Then, as
Mamá approached the tragic denouement of her story, I
was distracted by the sound of my Aunt Laura's violent
rocking. She seemed on the verge of tears. She knew the
fable was intended for her. That week she was going to
have her wedding gown fitted, though no firm date had
been set for the marriage. Mamá ignored Laura's obvious discomfort, digging out a ribbon from the sewing
basket she kept by her rocker while describing María's
long illness, "a fever that would not break for days."
She spoke of a mother's despair: "that woman climbed
the church steps on her knees every morning, wore only
black as a *promesa* to the Holy Virgin in exchange for
her daughter's health." By the time María returned
from her honeymoon with death, she was ravished, no
longer young or sane. "As you can see she is almost as
old as her mother already," Mamá lamented while tying
the ribbon to the ends of my hair, pulling it back with
such force that I just knew that I would never be able
to close my eyes completely again.

"That María is getting crazier every day." Mamá's
voice would take a lighter tone now, expressing satisfaction, either for the perfection of my braid, or for a story
well-told; it was hard to tell. "You know that tune she
is always humming?" Carried away by her enthusiasm,
I tried to nod, but Mamá would still have me pinned
between her knees.

"Well, that's the wedding march." Surprising us all,
Mamá sang out, "*Da, da, dará... da, da, dará.*" Then

lifting me off the floor by my skinny shoulders, she lead me around the room in an impromptu waltz—another session ending with the laughter of women, all of us caught up in the infectious joke of our lives.

The Woman Who Was Left at the Altar

She calls her shadow Juan,
looking back often as she walks.
She has grown fat, breasts huge
as reservoirs. She once opened her blouse
in church to show the silent town
what a plentiful mother she could be.
Since her old mother died, buried in black,
she lives alone.
Out of the lace she made curtains for her room,
doilies out of the veil. They are now
yellow as malaria.
She hangs live chickens from her waist to sell,
walks to the town swinging her skirts of flesh.
She doesn't speak to anyone. Dogs follow
the scent of blood to be shed. In their hungry,
yellow eyes she sees his face.
She takes him to the knife time after time.

More Room

My grandmother's house is like a chambered nautilus; it has many rooms, yet it is not a mansion. Its proportions are small and its design simple. It is a house that has grown organically, according to the needs of its inhabitants. To all of us in the family it is known as *la casa de Mamá.* It is the place of our origin; the stage for our memories and dreams of Island life.

I remember how in my childhood it sat on stilts; this was before it had a downstairs. It rested on its perch like a great blue bird, not a flying sort of bird, more like a nesting hen, but with spread wings. Grandfather had built it soon after their marriage. He was a painter and housebuilder by trade, a poet and meditative man by nature. As each of their eight children were born, new rooms were added. After a few years, the paint did not exactly match, nor the materials, so that there was a chronology to it, like the rings of a tree, and Mamá could tell you the history of each room in her *casa*, and thus the genealogy of the family along with it.

Her room is the heart of the house. Though I have seen it recently, and both woman and room have diminished in size, changed by the new perspective of my eyes, now capable of looking over countertops and tall beds, it is not this picture I carry in my memory of Mamá's *casa*. Instead, I see her room as a queen's chamber where a small woman loomed large, a throne-room with a massive four-poster bed in its center which stood taller than a child's head. It was on this bed where her own children had been born that the smallest grand-children were allowed to take naps in the afternoons; here too was where Mamá secluded herself to dispense private advice to her daughters, sitting on the edge of the bed, looking down at whoever sat on the rocker where generations of babies had been sung to sleep. To me she looked like a wise empress right out of the fairy tales I was addicted to reading.

Though the room was dominated by the mahogany four-poster, it also contained all of Mamá's symbols of power. On her dresser instead of cosmetics there were jars filled with herbs: *yerba buena, yerba mala*, the mak-ing of purgatives and teas to which we were all subjected during childhood crises. She had a steaming cup for anyone who could not, or would not, get up to face life on any given day. If the acrid aftertaste of her cures for malingering did not get you out of bed, then it was time to call *el doctor*.

And there was the monstrous chifforobe she kept locked with a little golden key she did not hide. This was a test of her dominion over us; though my cousins and I wanted a look inside that massive wardrobe more than anything, we never reached for that little key lying on top of her Bible on the dresser. This was also where she placed her earrings and rosary at night. God's word was her security system. This chifforobe was the place where I imagined she kept jewels, satin slippers, and elegant sequined, silk gowns of heartbreaking fineness. I lusted after those imaginary costumes. I had heard that Mamá had been a great beauty in her youth, and the belle of many balls. My cousins had other ideas as to what she kept in that wooden vault: its secret could be money (Mamá did not hand cash to strangers, banks were out of the question, so there were stories that her mattress was stuffed with dollar bills, and that she buried coins in jars in her garden under rosebushes, or kept them in her inviolate chifforobe); there might be that legendary gun salvaged from the Spanish-American conflict over the Island. We went wild over suspected treasures that we made up simply because children have to fill locked trunks with something wonderful.

On the wall above the bed hung a heavy silver crucifix. Christ's agonized head hung directly over Mamá's pillow. I avoided looking at this weapon suspended over where her head would lay; and on the rare occasions when I was allowed to sleep on that bed, I scooted down to the safe middle of the mattress, where her body's impression took me in like a mother's lap. Having taken care of the obligatory religious decoration with a crucifix, Mamá covered the other walls with objects sent to her over the years by her children in the States. *Los Nueva Yores* were represented by, among other things, a postcard of Niagara Falls from her son Hernán, postmarked, Buffalo, N.Y. In a conspicuous gold frame hung a large color photograph of her daughter Nena, her husband and their five children at the entrance to Disneyland in California. From us she had gotten a black lace fan. Father had brought it to her from a tour of duty with the Navy in Europe (on Sundays she would remove it from its hook on the wall to fan herself at mass). Each year more items were added as the family grew and dispersed, and every object in the room had a story attached to it, a *cuento* which Mamá would bestow on anyone who received the privilege of a day alone with her. It was almost worth pretending to be sick, though the bitter herb purgatives of the body were a big price to pay for the spirit revivals of her story-telling.

Mamá slept alone on her large bed, except for the times when a sick grandchild warranted the privilege, or when a heartbroken daughter came home in need of more than herbal teas. In the family there is a story about how this came to be.

When one of the daughters, my mother or one of her sisters, tells the *cuento* of how Mamá came to own her nights, it is usually preceded by the qualifications that Papá's exile from his wife's room was not a result of animosity between the couple, but that the act had been Mamá's famous bloodless coup for her personal freedom. Papá was the benevolent dictator of her body and her life who had had to be banished from her bed so that Mamá could better serve her family. Before the telling, we had to agree that the old man was not to blame. We all recognized that in the family Papá was as an *alma de Dios*, a saintly, soft-spoken presence whose main pleasures in life, such as writing poetry and reading the Spanish large-type editions of *Reader's Digest*, always took place outside the vortex of Mamá's crowded realm. It was not his fault, after all, that every year or so he planted a baby-seed in Mamá's fertile body, keeping her from leading the active life she needed and desired. He loved her and the babies. Papá composed odes and lyrics to celebrate births and anniversaries and hired musicians to accompany him in singing them to his family and friends at extravagant pig-roasts he threw yearly. Mamá and the oldest girls worked for days preparing the food. Papá sat for hours in his painter's shed, also his study and library, composing the songs. At these celebrations he was also known to give long speeches in praise of God, his fecund wife, and his beloved island. As a middle child, my mother remembers these occasions as a time when the women sat in the kitchen and lamented their burdens, while the men feasted out in the patio, their rum-thickened voices rising in song and praise for each other, *compañeros* all.

It was after the birth of her eighth child, after she had lost three at birth or in infancy, that Mamá made her decision. They say that Mamá had had a special way of letting her husband know that they were expecting, one that had begun when, at the beginning of their marriage, he had built her a house too confining for her taste. So, when she discovered her first pregnancy, she supposedly drew plans for another room, which he dutifully executed. Every time a child was due, she would demand, *more space, more space.* Papá acceded to her wishes, child after child, since he had learned early that Mamá's renowned temper was a thing that grew like a monster along with a new belly. In this way Mamá got the house that she wanted, but with each child she lost in heart and energy. She had knowledge of her body and perceived that if she had any more children, her dreams and her plans would have to be permanently forgotten, because she would be a chronically ill woman, like Flora with her twelve children: asthma, no teeth, in bed more than on her feet.

And so, after my youngest uncle was born, she asked Papá to build a large room at the back of the house. He did so in joyful anticipation. Mamá had asked him special things this time: shelves on the walls, a private entrance. He thought that she meant this room to be a nursery where several children could sleep. He thought it was a wonderful idea. He painted it his favorite color, sky blue, and made large windows looking out over a green hill and the church spires beyond. But nothing happened. Mamá's belly did not grow, yet she seemed in a frenzy of activity over the house. Finally, an anxious Papá approached his wife to tell her that the

new room was finished and ready to be occupied. And
Mamá, they say, replied: "Good, it's for *you*."

And so it was that Mamá discovered the only means
of birth control available to a Catholic woman of her
time: sacrifice. She gave up the comfort of Papá's sexual love for something she deemed greater: the right
to own and control her body, so that she might live to
meet her grandchildren—me among them—so that she
could give more of herself to the ones already there, so
that she could be more than a channel for other lives, so
that even now that time has robbed her of the elasticity
of her body and of her amazing reservoir of energy, she
still emanates the kind of joy that can only be achieved
by living according to the dictates of one's own heart.

Claims

Last time I saw her, Grandmother
had grown seamed as a bedouin tent.
She had claimed the right
to sleep alone, to own
her nights, to never bear
the weight of sex again, nor to accept
its gift of comfort, for the luxury
of stretching her bones.
She'd carried eight children,
three had sunk in her belly, *náufragos,*
she called them, shipwrecked babies
drowned in her black waters.
Children are made in the night and
steal your days
for the rest of your life, amen. She said this
to each of her daughters in turn. Once she had
    made a pact
with man and nature and kept it. Now like the sea,
she is claiming back her territory.

Talking to the Dead

My grandfather is a *Mesa Blanca* spiritist. This means that he is able to communicate with the spirit world. And since almost everyone has a request or complaint to make from the *Other Side*, Papá once was a much sought-after man in our pueblo. His humble demeanor and gentle ways did much to enhance his popularity with the refined matrons who much preferred to consult him than the rowdy *santeros* who, according to Papá, made a living through spectacle and the devil's arts. *Santería*, like voodoo, has its roots in African blood rites, which its devotees practice with great fervor. *Espiritismo*, on the other hand, entered the island via the middle classes who had discovered it flourishing in Europe during the so-called "crisis of faith" of the late nineteenth century. Poets like Yeats belonged to societies whose members sought answers in the invisible world. Papá, a poet and musician himself when he was not building houses, had the gift of clairvoyance, or *facultades*, as they are called in spiritism. It is not a free gift, however: being a spiritist medium requires living through *pruebas*, or tests of one's abilities.

Papá's most difficult *prueba* must have been living in the same house with Mamá, a practical woman who believed only in what her senses recorded. If Papá's eyes were closed that meant that her lazy man was sleeping in the middle of the day again. His visionary states and his poetry writing were, I have heard, the primary reasons why Mamá had, early in their married life, decided that her husband should "wear the pants" in the family only in the literal sense of the expression. She considered him a "hopeless case," a label she attached to any family member whose drive and energy did not match her own. She never changed her mind about his poetry writing, which she believed was Papá's perdition, the thing that kept him from making a fortune, but she learned to respect his *facultades* after the one incident that she could not easily dismiss or explain.

Although Papá had been building a reputation for many years as an effective medium, his gifts had not changed his position in Mamá's household. He had, at a time determined by his wife, been banished to the back of the house to pursue his interests, and as for family politics, his position was one of quiet assent with his wife's wise decisions. He could have rebelled against this situation: in Puerto Rican society, the man is considered a small-letter god in his home. But, Papá, a gentle, scholarly man, preferred a laissez-faire approach. Mamá's ire could easily be avoided by keeping his books and his spiritist practice out of her sight. And he did make a decent living designing and building houses.

In his room at the back of the house he dreamt his dreams and interpreted them. There he also received the spiritually needy: the recent widows, the women who had lost children, and the old ones who had started making plans for the afterlife. The voices were kept low during these consultations. I know from having sat in the hallway outside his door as a child, listening as hard as I could for what I thought should be taking place—howlings of the possessed, furniture being thrown around by angry ghosts—ideas I had picked up from such movies as *Abbot and Costello Meet the*

Mummy, and from misinterpreting the conversations of adults. But, Papá's seances were more like counseling sessions. Sometimes there were the sounds of a grown person sobbing—a frightening thing to a child—and then Papá's gentle, persuasive voice. Although most times I could not decipher the words, I recognized the tone of sympathy and support he was offering them. Two or more voices would at times join together in a chant. And the pungent odor of incense seeping through his closed door made my imagination quicken with visions of apparitions dancing above his table, waiting to speak through him to their loved ones. In a sort of trance myself, I would sometimes begin softly reciting an *Our Father*, responding automatically to the familiar experience of voices joined together in prayer and the church-smell of incense. What Papá performed in his room was a ceremony of healing. Whether he ever communicated with the dead I cannot say, but the spiritually wounded came to him and he tended to them and reassured them that death was not a permanent loss. He believed with all the passion of his poet's heart, and was able to convince others, that what awaits us all after the long day of our lives was a family reunion in God's extensive plantation. I believe he saw heaven as an island much like Puerto Rico, except without the inequities of backbreaking labor, loss and suffering which he could only justify to his followers as their prueba on this side of paradise.

Papá's greatest prueba came when his middle son, Hernán, disappeared. At the age of eighteen, Hernán had accepted a "free" ticket to the U.S. from a man recruiting laborers. It was a difficult time for the family, and reluctantly, Mamá had given Hernán permission to go. Papá, on the other hand, had uncharacteristically spoken out against the venture. He had had dreams, nightmares, in which he saw Hernán in prison, being tortured by hooded figures. Mamá dismissed his fears as fantasy-making, blaming Papá's premonitions on too much reading as usual. Hernán had been a wild teenager, and Mamá felt that it was time he became a working man. And so Hernán left the island, promising to write to his parents immediately, and was not heard from again for months.

Mamá went wild with worry. She imposed on friends and relatives, anyone who had a contact in the U.S., to join in the search for her son. She consulted with the police and with lawyers, and she even wrote to the governor, whose secretary wrote back that the recruiting of Puerto Rican laborers by mainland growers was being investigated by the authorities for the possibility of illegal practices. Mamá began to have nightmares herself in which she saw her son mistreated and worse. Papá stayed up with her during many of her desperate vigils. He said little, but kept his hands on his Bible, and would often seem to be speaking to himself in a trance. For once, Mamá did not ridicule him. She may have been too wrapped up in her despair. Then one night, Papá abruptly rose from his chair and rushed to his room where, with his carpenter's pencil, he began drawing something on the white cloth of his special table. Mamá followed him, thinking that her husband had gone mad with suffering for their child. But seeing the concentration on his face—it seemed to be lit with a light from within, she later told someone—she stood behind him for what seemed a long time. When he finished, he held a candle over the table and began explaining the picture as if to himself. "He is in a place far north. A place without a name. It is a place that can be found only by one who has been there. Here, there are growing things. Fruit, maybe. Sweet fruit. Not

ready to be picked yet. There are lights in the distance.
And a tall fence. Hernán sleeps here among the lights.
He is dreaming of me tonight. He is lonely and afraid,
but not sick or hurt."

Mamá began to see the things Papá described in the
rough pencil lines on that tablecloth. Her mind turned
into a map of memories, scraps of information, lines
from letters she had received over the years, Christmas
cards from strange places sent by a dozen nephews, or
the sons of neighbors—young men for whom she had
been a second mother—until she remembered this: a
few years before Hernán's departure, Alicia's (Mamá's
older sister) son, had also been "recruited" as a laborer.
Like Hernán, he had not been informed as to exactly
where he was going, only that it was in another Nueva
York, not the city. Unlike her own son, her nephew had
written home to say that he had been picking strawber-
ries and did not like the job. Soon after, he had moved
to a city near the farm where he had worked for a season. There he had married and settled down. Alicia
would know the name of the place. But Papá had said
it was a place without a name. Mamá decided to follow
up on the only premonition she had ever allowed into
her practical mind.

At that early hour, not quite dawn, the two of them
set out for the country, where Alicia lived; Papá was
armed with his Bible and the symbol of his calling: a
mahogany stick he had carved into a wand. Every spiritist must make one and take it with him on house calls.
It is hollow and sometimes filled with Holy Water in order to keep "evil influences" at a distance, but Papá had
put a handful of dirt from his birthplace in his, perhaps
because his calling as a medium was more than anything
a poet's choice of missions: a need to accept mortality
while struggling for permanence. Anyway, that earth-

filled stick was the only weapon I ever knew Papá to carry. That morning he and his wife walked together in silence, a rare occurrence: to Mamá, long silences were a vacuum her nature abhorred. They came home with hope in the form of a telephone number that day.

After sending for the high school English teacher to interpret, they called the city of Buffalo, New York. Mamá's nephew told them that he would start looking for Hernán at the farm right away. He said, everyone just called it "the farm."

It turned out that Hernán was at the farm. The situation was very bad. The workers had been brought there by an unscrupulous farm worker who kept the men (most of them very young and unable to speak English) ignorant as to their exact whereabouts. They lived in tents while they waited for the fruit to be ready for picking. Though they were given provisions, the cost was deducted from their paychecks, so by the time they were paid, their salary was already owed to the grower. The workers were told that mail was not picked up there and it would have to be taken to the nearest city after the harvest. Though Hernán and many of the other men protested their situation and threatened to strike, they knew that they were virtual prisoners and would have to wait for an opportunity to escape. Mamá's nephew had connections in Buffalo and was able to convince a social worker to accompany him to the farm where he found Hernán eager to lead the exodus. It was not as easy as that, though. Many days passed before an investigation was started which revealed the scheme behind the farm and many others like it based on the recruitment of young men under false pretenses. But Hernán had been found. And Mamá learned to respect, if not quite ever to publicly acknowledge, her husband's gift of clairvoyance.

She paid her tribute to him in her own way by em-
broidering a new cloth for his *mesa blanca* in a pattern
based on his drawings of that night. She did it with
white thread on white cloth, so that to see it one had to
get very close to the design.

Housepainter

The flecks are deeply etched
into the creases of his fingers,
and the paint will not wash off.
It was a hilltop house he painted last
for an old woman going blind
who wanted it to blend into the sky.
It took him two weeks working alone,
and the blue, a hue too dark,
stood out against the horizon
like a storm cloud, but since clouds
had also gathered over her eyes,
she never knew.
He explained his life to me,
a child on my grandfather's lap
concerned with his speckled hands only because
they kept me from my treasure hunting
in his painter's shed, where cans on shelves
spilled enamel over their lids
like tears running down a clown's face.

① women's role
② Maturity
③ Men's role

The Black Virgin

In their wedding photograph my parents look like children dressed in adult costumes. And they are. My mother will not be fifteen years old for two weeks; she has borrowed a wedding dress from a relative, a tall young woman recently widowed by the Korean war. For sentimental reasons they have chosen not to alter the gown, and it hangs awkwardly on my mother's thin frame. The tiara is crooked on her thick black curls because she had bumped her head coming out of the car. On her face is a slightly stunned, pouty expression, as if she were considering bursting into tears. At her side stands my father, formal in his high-school graduation suit. He is holding her elbow as the photographer has instructed him to do; he looks myopically straight ahead since he is not wearing his wire-frame glasses. His light brown curls frame his cherubic, well-scrubbed face; his pale, scholarly appearance contrasts with his bride's sultry beauty, dark skin and sensuous features. Neither one seems particularly interested in the other. They are posing reluctantly. The photograph will be evidence that a real wedding took place. I arrived more than a year later, so it was not a forced wedding. In fact, both families had opposed the marriage for a number of reasons only to discover how adamant children in love can be.

My parents' families represented two completely op-

38

posite cultural and philosophical lines of ancestry in my hometown. My maternal relatives, said to have originally immigrated from Italy, were all farmers. My earliest memories are imbued with the smell of dark, moist earth and the image of red coffee beans growing row after row on my great-grandfather's hillside farm. On my father's side there is family myth and decadence. His people had come from Spain bringing tales of wealth and titles, but all I was aware of as a child was that my grandfather had died of alcoholism and meanness a few months before my birth, and that he had forbidden his wife and children ever to mention his family background in his house, under threat of violence.

My father was a quiet, serious man; my mother, earthy and ebullient. Their marriage, like my childhood, was the combining of two worlds, the mixing of two elements—fire and ice. This was sometimes exciting and life-giving and sometimes painful and draining.

Because their early marriage precluded many options for supporting a wife, and because they had a child on the way, father joined the U.S. Army only few months after the wedding. He was promptly shipped to Panama, where he was when I was born, and where he stayed for the next two years. I have seen many pictures of myself, a pampered infant and toddler, taken during those months for his benefit. My mother lived with his mother and learned to wait and to smoke. My father's two older brothers were in Korea during the same period of time.

My mother still talks nostalgically of those years when she lived with Mamá Nanda, as her grandchildren called her, since her name, Fernanda, was beyond our ability to pronounce during our early years. Mamá Nanda's divorced daughter, my aunt Felícita, whom I am said to resemble, also lived with us. The three women living alone and receiving Army checks were the envy of every married woman in the pueblo.

My mother had been the fourth child in a family of eight, and had spent most of her young life caring for babies that came one after the other until her mother had exiled her husband from her bed. Mamá Pola had been six months pregnant with her last child at my parents' wedding. My mother had been resentful and embarrassed about her mother's condition, and this may have had some effect on my grandmother's decision.

Anyway, my mother relished the grown-up atmosphere at her mother-in-law's house, where Mamá Nanda was beginning to experiment with a new sense of personal freedom since her husband's death of alcohol-related causes a couple of years before. Though bound by her own endless rituals of religion and superstition, she had allowed herself a few pleasures. Chief among these was cigarette smoking. For years, the timid wife and overworked mother had sneaked a smoke behind the house as she worked in her herb garden where she astutely grew mint to chew on before entering the house. Occasionally she would steal a Chesterfield from her husband's coat pocket while he slept in a drunken stupor. Now she bought them by the carton, and one could always detect the familiar little square in her apron pocket. My mother took up the smoking habit enthusiastically. And she, my aunt Felícita and Mamá Nanda spent many lazy afternoons smoking and talking about life—especially about the travails of having lived with the old man who had been disinherited by his father at an early age for drinking and gambling, and who had allowed bitterness for his bad fortune to further dissipate him. They told family stories, stories which moralized or amused according to whether it was Mamá Nanda or the New York-sophisticated Felícita who told them. They were stories my mother would later repeat to me to pass the time away in colder climates while she waited to return to her island. My mother never adopted the U.S., she did not adapt to life anywhere but in Puerto Rico, although she followed my father back and forth from the island to the mainland for 25 years according to his tours of duty with the Navy. She always expected to return to *Casa*—her birthplace. And she kept her fantasy alive by recounting her early years to my brother and me until we felt that we had shared her childhood.

At her mother-in-law's, Mother learned the meaning of scandal. She considered the gossip created by Felícita's divorce in New York and subsequent return to the conservative Catholic pueblo yet another exciting dimension in her new adventure of marriage. After her young husband had left for Panama, she had had trouble sleeping, so Aunt Felícita had offered to sleep in the same bed with her. Felícita had desperately wanted a child of her own, but her body had rejected three atempts at pregnancy—one of the many problems that had helped to destroy her marriage. And so my mother's condition became Felícita's project; she liked to say that she felt like the baby was hers too. After all, it was she who had felt the first stirrings in my mother's belly as she soothed the nervous girl through difficult nights, and she who had risen at dawn to hold her up while she heaved with morning-sickness. She shared the pregnancy, growing ever closer to the pretty girl carrying her brother's child.

She had also been the one to run out of the house in her nightgown one night in February of 1952 to summon the old midwife, Lupe, because it was time for me to make my entrance into the world. Lupe, who had attended at each of Mamá Nanda's twelve deliveries,

was by that time more a town institution than an alert
midwife. That night she managed to pull me out of
my mother's writhing body without serious complica-
tions, but it had exhausted her. She left me wrapped
up in layers of gauze without securing my umbilicus. It
was Felícita, ever vigilant of her babies, my mother and
myself, who spotted the blood stain soaking through my
swaddling clothes. I was rapidly emptying out, deflating
like a little balloon even as my teenage mother curled
into a fetal position to sleep after her long night's work.

They say that until my father's return, the social
pariah, Felícita, cared for me with a gentle devotion
that belied all her outward bravura. Some years before my birth, she had eloped with a young man whom
her father had threatened to kill. They had married and
gone to New York City to live. During that time, all her
letters home had been destroyed in their envelopes by
the old man who had pronounced her dead to the family. Mamá Nanda had suffered in silence, but managed
to keep in touch with her daughter through a relative in
New York. The marriage soon disintegrated and Felícita
explored life as a free woman for one year. Her exploits,
exaggerated by gossip, made her legendary in her hometown. By the time I could ask about such things, all
that was left of that period was a trunk full of gorgeous
party dresses Felícita had brought back. They became
my dress-up costumes during my childhood. She had
been a striking girl with the pale skin and dark curly
hair that my father's family could trace back to their
ancestors from northern Spain.

Piecing her story together over the years, I have
gathered that Felícita, at the age of sixteen, had fallen
madly in love with a black boy a little older than herself. The romance was passionate and the young man
had pressed for a quick marriage. When he finally ap-

proached my grandfather, the old man pulled out his machete and threatened to cut Felícita's suitor in half with it if he ever came near the house again. He then beat both his daugher and wife (for raising a slut), and put them under house-arrest. The result of his actions was an elopment in which half the town collaborated, raising money for the star-crossed lovers and helping them secure transportation and airline tickets to New York. Felícita left one night and did not return for many years after her father's death.

But the tale is more complex than that. There was talk at the time that the groom may have been fathered by the old man, who kept mistresses but did not acknowledge their children. For his pleasure, he nearly always chose black women. There was no way to prove this awful suspicion one way or another. Felícita had been struck and blinded by a passion that she could not control. The marriage had been tempestuous, violent, and mercifully short. Felícita was a wounded person by the time I was born; her fire was no longer raging, but smoldering—just enough to keep me warm until my mother came out of her adolescent dream to take charge of me.

The three women and a baby girl then spent the next two years waiting for their soldier to come home. Mamá Nanda, a deeply religious woman, as well as superstitious, made a *promesa* for the safe return of her three sons. She went to early mass every day at the famous Catholic church in our town, the site of a miraculous appearance by the Black Virgin during the Spanish colonial period. Mamá Nanda also climbed the one hundred steps to the shrine on her knees once a week, along with other women who had men in the war. These steps had been hewn out of a hillside by hundreds of laborers, and a church had been constructed at the top, on the exact spot where a woodcutter had been saved from a charging bull by the sudden vision of the Black Lady floating above a treetop. According to legend, the bull fell on its front knees in a dead halt right in front of the man paralyzed by fear and wonder. There is a fresco above the church altar depicting this scene. Pilgrims come from all over the island to visit the shrine of the Black Virgin. A statue imported from Spain representing the Lady sits on a portable ark, and once a year, during her *Fiestas Patronales*, she is taken on her dais around the town, followed by her adorers. She is said to have effected many miraculous cures, and her little room, off to the side of the nave, is full of mementos of her deeds, such as crutches and baby garments (she can induce fertility in barren women). It was to her that Mamá Nanda and other women prayed when their men were in wars and during domestic crises. Being a woman and black made Our Lady the perfect depository for the hopes and prayers of the sick, the weak and the powerless.

I have seen the women dressed in black climbing the rough steps of *La Escalinata* to the front portals of the church and I have understood how the act itself could bring comfort to a woman who did not even know exactly where on earth her son or husband was, or even the reasons why he was risking his life in someone else's war. Perhaps God knew, and surely Our Lady, a woman, wife, and mother herself, would intercede. It was a man's world, and a man's heaven. But mediation was possible—if one could only get *His* attention. And so there were *promesas*, ways to make your requests noticed. Some women chose to wear *hábitos* until their prayers were answered, that is, a plain dress of the color that represented their favorite saint, such as light blue for the Holy Mother or red for the Sa-

cred Heart. The *hábito* was cinched at the waist with
a cord representing Christ's passion. The more fer-
vent would wear sackcloth underneath their clothes, a
real torment in the tropical heat. The *promesa* was
only limited by the imagination of the penitent and
her threshold for pain and discomfort. In many house-
holds women said rosaries nightly in groups, and this
brought them together to share in their troubles. Mamá
Nanda did it all, quietly and without fanfare. She wore
only black since the death of her husband, but mourn-
ing and penance had become an intrinsic part of her
nature long before; of her twelve children only six had
survived; the other six died in infancy from childhood
diseases which were prevented a generation later by a
single vaccine or simple antidote. She had buried each
little corpse in the family graveyard with a name and
a date on the headstone—sometimes the same date for
birth and death—and she had worn black, kept *luto* for
each. The death of her babies had made her a melancholy woman, yet one who was always ready to give
God another chance. She lobbied for His favors inde-
fatigably.

At Mamá Nanda's house, my young mother and
her baby were treated like royalty. Having served a
demanding husband and numerous children, the older
woman now found herself in a practically empty house
with a new grandchild she could dote on and a daugher-
in-law that was no more than an adolescent herself. My
mother's only job was to play with the baby, to take me
for strolls in fancy clothes bought with Army checks,
and to accompany Mamá Nanda to mass on Sundays.
In the photographs taken of my mother and me during
this period, I can see the changes wrought on the shy
teenage bride in the short span she was taken care of
by Nanda and Felícita: she is chubby and radiant with

good health, she seems proud of the bundle of ruffles
and bows in her arms—her babydoll—me.

By the time Father returned from Panama, I was
out of diapers and ambulatory, Mother had regained
her svelte figure, and Mamá Nanda had thick calluses
on her knees which kept her from feeling the pain she
thought was necessary to get results from heaven. The
safe homecoming of her son was proof that her sacrifices
had been worthwhile, and she applied her fruitful mind
to even greater penances toward credit for the other two
who would both be wounded in an ambush while traveling in a jeep in Korea and would soon be back in Puerto
Rico—slightly damaged, but alive. Nanda's knees bore
the scars like medals received in many wars and con-
flicts. Aunt Felícita found herself suddenly displaced as
my "other parent," and returned to her own life. All
changed.

My first memory is of Father's homecoming party
and the gift he brought me from San Juan—a pink iron
crib like an ornate bird cage—and the sense of abandonment I felt for the first time in my short life as all
eyes turned to the handsome stranger in uniform and
away from me in my frilly new dress and patent leather
shoes, trapped inside my pink iron crib, screaming my
head off for *Mami, Tía, Mamá Nanda,* anybody ... to
come lift me out of my prison.

When I ask about the events of that day, my mother
still rolls her eyes back and throws her hands up in a
gesture of dismay. The story varies with the telling and
the teller, but it seems that I climbed out of my tall crib
on my own and headed for the party in the backyard.
The pig was on the spit and the beer was flowing. In
the living room the Victrola was playing my father's
Elvis Presley records loudly. *I may have imagined this.*
My mother is sitting on his lap. She is gorgeous in

the red silk dress he has given her. There is a circle of people around him. Everyone is having a good time. And everyone has forgotten about me. I see myself slipping through the crowd and into flames. Immediately, I am pulled out by a man's strong hands. No real damage: my abundant hair is a little singed, but that is all. Mother is crying. I am the center of everyone's attention once again. Even *his*. Did I sleep between them that night because my mother had finally realized that I was not a rubber dolly but a real flesh and blood little girl? When I ask, she says that she remembers only staying awake listening to me breathe on the night of "the incident." She had also been kept up by the unaccustomed noise of my father's snoring. She would soon get used to both facts of life: that every one of her waking hours would belong to me from then on, and that this solemn stranger—who only resembled the timid young man she had married two years before—would own her nights. My mother was finally coming of age.

They Say

They say
when I arrived,
traveling light,
the women who waited
plugged
the cracks in the walls
with rags
dipped in alcohol
to keep drafts and demons out.
Candles were lit
to the Virgin.
They say
Mother's breath
kept blowing them out
right and left.
When I slipped
into their hands
the room was in shadows.
They say
I nearly turned away,
undoing
the hasty knot of my umbilicus.
They say
my urge to bleed
told them I was like a balloon
with a leak,

a soul trying to fly away
through the cracks in the wall.
The midwife sewed
and the women prayed
as they fitted
me for life
in a tight corset of gauze.
But their prayers
held me back,
the bandages held me in,
and all that night
they dipped
their bloody rags.
They say
Mother slept through it all,
blowing out
candles
with her breath.

Quinceañera

My dolls have been put away like dead
children in a chest I will carry
with me when I marry.
I reach under my skirt to feel
a satin slip bought for this day. It is soft
as the inside of my thighs. My hair
has been nailed back with my mother's
black hairpins to my skull. Her hands
stretched my eyes open as she twisted
braids into a tight circle at the nape
of my neck. I am to wash my own clothes
and sheets from this day on, as if
the fluids of my body were poison, as if
the little trickle of blood I believe
travels from my heart to the world were
shameful. Is not the blood of saints and
men in battle beautiful? Do Christ's hands
not bleed into your eyes from His cross?
At night I hear myself growing and wake
to find my hands drifting of their own will
to soothe skin stretched tight
over my bones.
I am wound like the guts of a clock,
waiting for each hour to release me.

Primary Lessons

My mother walked me to my first day at school at La Escuela Segundo Ruiz Belvis, named after the Puerto Rican patriot born in our town. I remember yellow cement with green trim. All the classrooms had been painted these colors to identify them as government property. This was true all over the Island. Everything was color-coded, including the children, who wore uniforms from first through twelfth grade. We were a midget army in white and brown, led by the hand to our battleground. From practically every house in our barrio emerged a crisply ironed uniform inhabited by the savage creatures we had become over a summer of running wild in the sun.

At my grandmother's house where we were staying until my father returned to Brooklyn Yard in New York and sent for us, it had been complete chaos, with several children to get ready for school. My mother had pulled my hair harder than usual while braiding it, and I had dissolved into a pool of total self-pity. I wanted to stay home with her and Mamá, to continue listening to stories in the late afternoon, to drink *café con leche* with them, and to play rough games with my many cousins. I wanted to continue living the dream of summer afternoons in Puerto Rico, and if I could not have it, then I wanted to go back to Paterson, New Jersey, back to where I imagined our apartment waited, peaceful and cool, for the three of us to return to our former lives. Our gypsy lifestyle had convinced me, at age six, that one part of life stops and waits for you while you live another for a while—and if you don't like the present, you can always return to the past. Buttoning me into my stiff blouse while I tried to squirm away from her, my mother attempted to explain to me that I was a big girl now and should try to understand that, like all the other children my age, I had to go to school.

"What about him?" I yelled pointing at my brother who was lounging on the tile floor of our bedroom in his pajamas, playing quietly with a toy car.

"He's too young to go to school, you know that. Now stay still." My mother pinned me between her thighs to button my skirt, as she had learned to do from Mamá, from whose grip it was impossible to escape.

"It's not fair, it's not fair. I can't go to school here. I don't speak Spanish." It was my final argument, and it failed miserably because I was shouting my defiance in the language I claimed not to speak. Only I knew what I meant by saying in Spanish that I did not speak Spanish. I had spent my early childhood in the U.S. where I lived in a bubble created by my Puerto Rican parents in a home where two cultures and languages became one. I learned to listen to the English from the television with one ear while I heard my mother and father speaking in Spanish with the other. I thought I was an ordinary American kid—like the children on the shows I watched—and that everyone's parents spoke a secret second language at home. When we came to Puerto Rico right before I started first grade, I switched easily to Spanish. It was the language of fun, of summertime games. But school—that was a different matter.

I made one last desperate effort to make my mother see reason: "Father will be very angry. You know that

he wants us to speak good English." My mother, of
course, ignored me as she dressed my little brother in
his playclothes. I could not believe her indifference to
my father's wishes. She was usually so careful about
our safety and the many other areas that he was forever reminding her about in his letters. But I was right,
and she knew it. Our father spoke to us in English as
much as possible, and he corrected my pronunciation
constantly—not "jes" but "y-es." Y-es, sir. How could
she send me to school to learn Spanish when we would
be returning to Paterson in just a few months?

But, of course, what I feared was not language, but
loss of freedom. At school there would be no playing,
no stories, only lessons. It would not matter if I did not
understand a word, and I would not be allowed to make
up my own definitions. I would have to learn silence.
I would have to keep my wild imagination in check.
Feeling locked into my stiffly starched uniform, I only
sensed all this. I guess most children can intuit their loss
of childhood's freedom on that first day of school. It is
separation anxiety too, but mother is just the guardian
of the "playground" of our early childhood.

The sight of my cousins in similar straits comforted
me. We were marched down the hill of our barrio where
Mamá's robin-egg-blue house stood at the top. I must
have glanced back at it with yearning. Mamá's house—
a place built for children—where anything that could be
broken had already been broken by my grandmother's
early batch of offspring (they ranged in age from my
mother's oldest sisters to my uncle who was six months
older than me.) Her house had long since been made
child-proof. It had been a perfect summer place. And
now it was September—the cruelest month for a child.

La Mrs., as all the teachers were called, waited for
her class of first-graders at the door of the yellow and

green classroom. She too wore a uniform: it was a blue skirt and a white blouse. This teacher wore black high heels with her "standard issue." I remember this detail because when we were all seated in rows she called on one little girl and pointed to the back of the room where there were shelves. She told the girl to bring her a shoebox from the bottom shelf. Then, when the box had been placed in her hands, she did something unusual. She had the little girl kneel at her feet and take the pointy high heels off her feet and replace them with a pair of satin slippers from the shoe box. She told the group that every one of us would have a chance to do this if we behaved in her class. Though confused about the prize, I soon felt caught up in the competition to bring *La Mrs.* her slippers in the morning. Children fought over the privilege.

Our first lesson was English. In Puerto Rico, every child has to take twelve years of English to graduate from school. It is the law. In my parents' schooldays, all subjects were taught in English. The U.S. Department of Education had specified that as a U.S. territory, the Island had to be "Americanized," and to accomplish this task, it was necessary for the Spanish language to be replaced in one generation through the teaching of English in all schools. My father began his school day by saluting the flag of the United States and singing "America" and "The Star-Spangled Banner" by rote, without understanding a word of what he was saying. The logic behind this system was that, though the children did not understand the English words, they would remember the rhythms. Even the games the teacher's manuals required them to play became absurd adaptations. "Here We Go Round the Mulberry Bush" became "Here We Go Round the Mango Tree." I have heard about the confusion caused by the use of a primer in which the sounds of animals were featured. The children were forced to accept that a rooster says *cockadoodledoo*, when they knew perfectly well from hearing their own roosters each morning that in Puerto Rico a rooster says *cocorocó*. Even the vocabulary of their pets was changed; there are still family stories circulating about the bewilderment of a first-grader coming home to try to teach his dog to speak in English. The policy of assimilation by immersion failed on the Island. Teachers adhered to it on paper, substituting their own materials for the texts, but no one took their English home. In due time, the program was minimized to the one class in English per day that I encountered when I took my seat in *La Mrs.*'s first grade class.

Catching us all by surprise, she stood very straight and tall in front of us and began to sing in English:

"Pollito — Chicken
Gallina — Hen
Lápiz — Pencil
Y Pluma — Pen."

"Repeat after me, children: Pollito—Chicken," she commanded in her heavily accented English that only I understood, being the only child in the room who had ever been exposed to the language. But I too remained silent. No use making waves, or showing off. Patiently *La Mrs.* sang her song and gestured for us to join in. At some point it must have dawned on the class that this silly routine was likely to go on all day if we did not "repeat after her." It was not her fault that she had to follow the rule in her teacher's manual stating that she must teach English *in* English, and that she must not translate, but merely repeat her lesson in English until the children "begin to respond" more or less "unconsciously." This was one of the vestiges of the regimen followed by her predecessors in the last generation. To this day I can recite "Pollito—Chicken" mindlessly, never once pausing to visualize chicks, hens, pencils, or pens.

I soon found myself crowned "teacher's pet" without much effort on my part. I was a privileged child in her eyes simply because I lived in "Nueva York," and because my father was in the Navy. His name was an old one in our pueblo, associated with once-upon-a-time landed people and long-gone money. Status is judged by unique standards in a culture where, by definition, everyone is a second-class citizen. Remembrance of past glory is as good as titles and money. Old families living in decrepit old houses rank over factory workers living in modern comfort in cement boxes—all the same. The professions raise a person out of the dreaded "sameness" into a niche of status, so that teachers, nurses, and everyone who went to school for a job were given the honorifics of *El Míster* or *La Mrs.* by the common folks, people who were likely to be making more money in American factories than the poorly paid educators and government workers.

My first impressions of the hierarchy began with my teacher's shoe-changing ceremony and the exaggerated respect she received from our parents. *La Mrs.* was always right, and adults scrambled to meet her requirements. She wanted all our schoolbooks covered in the brown paper now used for paperbags (used at that time by the grocer to wrap meats and other foods). That first week of school the grocer was swamped with requests for paper which he gave away to the women. That week and the next, he wrapped produce in newspapers. All school projects became family projects. It was considered disrespectful at Mamá's house to do homework in privacy. Between the hours when we came home from school and dinner time, the table was shared by all of us working together with the women hovering in the background. The teachers communicated directly with the mothers, and it was a matriarchy of far-reaching power and influence.

There was a black boy in my first-grade classroom who was also the teacher's pet but for a different reason than I: I did not have to do anything to win her favor; he would do anything to win a smile. He was as black as the cauldron that Mamá used for cooking stew and his hair was curled into tight little balls on his head—*pasitas*, like little raisins glued to his skull, my mother had said. There had been some talk at Mamá's house about this boy; Lorenzo was his name. I later gathered that he was the grandson of my father's nanny. Lorenzo lived with Teresa, his grandmother, having been left in her care when his mother took off for "Los Nueva Yores" shortly after his birth. And they were poor. Everyone could see that his pants were too big for him—hand-me-downs—and his shoe soles were as thin as paper. Lorenzo seemed unmindful of the giggles he caused when he jumped up to erase the board for *La Mrs.* and his baggy pants rode down to his thin hips as he strained up to get every stray mark. He seemed to relish playing the little clown when she asked him to come to the front of the room and sing his phonetic version of "obootifool, forpashios-keeis" leading the class in our incomprehensible tribute to the American flag. He was a bright, loving child, with a talent for song and mimicry that everyone commented on. He should have been chosen to host the PTA show that year instead of me.

At recess one day, I came back to the empty classroom to get something, my cup? My nickel for a drink from the kioskman? I don't remember. But I remember the conversation my teacher was having with another teacher. I remember because it concerned me, and because I memorized it so that I could ask my mother to explain what it meant.

"He is a funny *negrito,* and, like a parrot, he can repeat anything you teach him. But his Mamá must not have the money to buy him a suit."

"I kept Rafaelito's First Communion suit; I bet Lorenzo could fit in it. It's white with a bow-tie," the other teacher said.

"But, Marisa," laughed my teacher, "in that suit, Lorenzo would look like a fly drowned in a glass of milk."

Both women laughed. They had not seen me crouched at the back of the room, digging into my schoolbag. My name came up then.

"What about the Ortiz girl? They have money."

"I'll talk to her mother today. The superintendent, *El Americano* from San Juan, is coming down for the show. How about if we have her say her lines in both Spanish and English."

The conversation ends there for me. My mother took me to Mayagüez and bought me a frilly pink dress and two crinoline petticoats to wear underneath so that I looked like a pink and white parachute with toothpick legs sticking out. I learned my lines, "Padres, maestros, Mr. Leonard, bienvenidos/Parents, teachers, Mr. Leonard, welcome ... " My first public appearance. I took no pleasure in it. The words were formal and empty. I had simply memorized them. My dress pinched me at the neck and arms, and made me itch all over.

I had asked my mother what it meant to be a "mosca en un vaso de leche," a fly in a glass of milk. She had laughed at the image, explaining that it meant being "different," but that it wasn't something I needed to worry about.

Christmas, 1961

We are waiting out the year with Mother's relatives
in Puerto Rico. Costumed as an angel for the play
at La Escuela San José, I am posing
in a white-sheet robe and tissue-paper wings
for my mother—a photo she will send
to my father who is at sea. Soon
he will be lost to us for months,
held in silence within his navy ship,
by a mistake and a gamble:
The Bay of Pigs, the Missile Crisis.
                                        The background
she chooses for me is a tropical tapestry: a hedge
of hibiscus, insistent scarlet
on a field of green. In the exposed print,
the flowers will bleed at the edges
of my ghostly shape—a fake angel
superimposed on a fake Eden,
as suspect as the hand-colored photogravures
in *National Geographics* during the war years,
showing "emerald forests and azure seas."

>   *Who knows how fear can change the face*
>   *of everything? The colors*
>   *of a picture left in an empty house*
>   *will fade to yellow. The paper*
>   *will cocoon around a moment*
>   *in a reversed metamorphosis.*

She had his last letter in the pocket
of her yellow dress—a *We will be together soon* note

she will carry with her for weeks like a talisman.
"Look at me," she says, and I am nearly blinded
by her radiance. That day she had swallowed the
    sun.
I lower my eyes to the box camera aimed at me,
and in the eye of the lens I can see

a tiny world burning.

One More Lesson

I remember Christmas on the Island by the way it felt on my skin. The temperature dropped into the ideal seventies and even lower after midnight when some of the more devout Catholics—mostly older women—got up to go to church, *misa del gallo* they called it; mass at the hour when the rooster crowed for Christ. They would drape shawls over their heads and shoulders and move slowly toward town. The birth of Our Savior was a serious affair in our *pueblo*.

At Mamá's house, food was the focal point of *Navidad*. There were banana leaves brought in bunches by the boys, spread on the table, where the women would pour coconut candy steaming hot, and the leaves would wilt around the sticky lumps, adding an extra tang of flavor to the already irresistible treat. Someone had to watch the candy while it cooled, or it would begin to disappear as the children risked life and limb for a stolen piece of heaven. The banana leaves were also used to wrap the traditional food of holidays in Puerto Rico: *pasteles*, the meat pies made from grated yucca and plantain and stuffed with spiced meats.

Every afternoon during the week before Christmas Day, we would come home from school to find the women sitting around in the parlor with bowls on their laps, grating pieces of coconut, yuccas, plantains, cheeses—all the ingredients that would make up our

Christmas Eve feast. The smells that filled Mamá's house at that time have come to mean anticipation and a sensual joy during a time in my life, the last days of my early childhood, when I could still absorb joy through my pores—when I had not yet learned that light is followed by darkness, that all of creation is based on that simple concept, and maturity is a discovery of that natural law.

It was in those days that the Americans sent baskets of fruit to our barrio—apples, oranges, grapes flown in from the States. And at night, if you dared to walk up to the hill where the mango tree stood in the dark, you could see a wonderful sight: a Christmas tree, a real pine, decorated with lights of many colors. It was the blurry outline of this tree you saw, for it was inside a screened-in-porch, but we had heard a thorough description of it from the boy who delivered the fruit, a nephew of Mamá's, as it had turned out. Only, I was not impressed, since just the previous year we had put up a tree ourselves in our apartment in Paterson.

Packages arrived for us in the mail from our father. I got dolls dressed in the national costumes of Spain, Italy, and Greece (at first we could not decide which of the Greek dolls was the male, since they both wore skirts); my brother got picture books; and my mother, jewelry that she would not wear, because it was too much like showing off and might attract the Evil Eye.

Evil Eye or not, the three of us were the envy of the pueblo. Everything about us set us apart, and I put away my dolls quickly when I discovered that my playmates would not be getting any gifts until *Los Reyes*—the Day of the Three Kings, when Christ received His gifts—and that even then it was more likely that the gifts they found under their beds would be practical things like clothes. Still, it was fun to find fresh grass for the camels the night the Kings were expected, tie it in bundles with string, and put it under our beds along with a bowl of fresh water.

The year went by fast after Christmas, and in the spring we received a telegram from Father. His ship had arrived in Brooklyn Yard. He gave us a date for our trip back to the States. I remember Mother's frantic packing, and the trips to Mayagüez for new clothes; the inspections of my brother's and my bodies for cuts, scrapes, mosquito bites, and other "damage" she would have to explain to Father. And I remember begging Mamá to tell me stories in the afternoons, although it was not summer yet and the trips to the mango tree had not begun. In looking back I realize that Mamá's stories were what I packed—my winter store.

Father had succeeded in finding an apartment outside Paterson's "vertical barrio," the tenement Puerto Ricans called *El Building*. He had talked a Jewish candy store owner into renting us the apartment above his establishment, which he and his wife had just vacated after buying a house in West Paterson, an affluent suburb. Mr. Schultz was a nice man whose melancholy face I was familiar with from trips I had made often with my father to his store for cigarettes. Apparently, my father had convinced him and his brother, a lookalike of Mr. Schultz who helped in the store, that we were not the usual Puerto Rican family. My father's fair skin, his ultra-correct English, and his Navy uniform were a good argument. Later it occurred to me that my father had been displaying me as a model child when he took me to that store with him. I was always dressed as if for church and held firmly by the hand. I imagine he did the same with my brother. As for my mother, her Latin beauty, her thick black hair that hung to her waist, her voluptuous body which even the win-

ter clothes could not disguise, would have been nothing but a hindrance to my father's plans. But everyone knew that a Puerto Rican woman is her husband's
satellite; she reflects both his light and his dark sides.
If my father was respectable, then his family would be
respectable. We got the apartment on Park Avenue.

Unlike El Building, where we had lived on our first
trip to Paterson, our new home was truly in exile. There
were Puerto Ricans by the hundreds only one block
away, but we heard no Spanish, no loud music, no mothers yelling at children, nor the familiar *¡Ay Bendito!*,
that catch-all phrase of our people. Mother lapsed into
silence herself, suffering from *La Tristeza*, the sadness
that only place induces and only place cures. But Father relished silence, and we were taught that silence
was something to be cultivated and practiced.

Since our apartment was situated directly above
where the Schultzes worked all day, our father instructed us to remove our shoes at the door and walk in
our socks. We were going to prove how respectable we
were by being the opposite of what our ethnic group was
known to be—we would be quiet and inconspicuous.

I was escorted each day to school by my nervous
mother. It was a long walk in the cooling air of fall
in Paterson and we had to pass by El Building where
the children poured out of the front door of the di-
lapidated tenement still answering their mothers in a
mixture of Spanish and English: "Sí, Mami, I'll come
straight home from school." At the corner we were
halted by the crossing guard, a strict woman who only
gestured her instructions, never spoke directly to the
children, and only ordered us to "halt" or "cross" while
holding her white-gloved hand up at face level or swinging her arm sharply across her chest if the light was
green.

The school building was not a welcoming sight for someone used to the bright colors and airiness of tropical architecture. The building looked functional. It could have been a prison, an asylum, or just what it was: an urban school for the children of immigrants, built to withstand waves of change, generation by generation. Its red brick sides rose to four solid stories. The black steel fire escapes snaked up its back like an exposed vertebra. A chain-link fence surrounded its concrete playground. Members of the elite safety patrol, older kids, sixth graders mainly, stood at each of its entrances, wearing their flourescent white belts that criss-crossed their chests and their metal badges. No one was allowed in the building until the bell rang, not even on rainy or bitter-cold days. Only the safety-patrol stayed warm.

My mother stood in front of the main entrance with me and a growing crowd of noisy children. She looked like one of us, being no taller than the six-grade girls. She held my hand so tightly that my fingers cramped. When the bell rang, she walked me into the building and kissed my cheek. Apparently my father had done all the paperwork for my enrollment, because the next thing I remember was being led to my third-grade classroom by a black girl who had emerged from the principal's office.

Though I had learned some English at home during my first years in Paterson, I had let it recede deep into my memory while learning Spanish in Puerto Rico. Once again I was the child in the cloud of silence, the one who had to be spoken to in sign language as if she were a deaf-mute. Some of the children even raised their voices when they spoke to me, as if I had trouble hearing. Since it was a large troublesome class composed mainly of black and Puerto Rican children, with a few working-class Italian children interspersed, the teacher paid little attention to me. I re-learned the language quickly by the immersion method. I remember one day, soon after I joined the rowdy class when our regular teacher was absent and Mrs. D., the sixth-grade teacher from across the hall, attempted to monitor both classes. She scribbled something on the chalkboard and went to her own room. I felt a pressing need to use the bathroom and asked Julio, the Puerto Rican boy who sat behind me, what I had to do to be excused. He said that Mrs. D. had written on the board that we could be excused by simply writing our names under the sign. I got up from my desk and started for the front of the room when I was struck on the head hard with a book. Startled and hurt, I turned around expecting to find one of the bad boys in my class, but it was Mrs. D. I faced. I remember her angry face, her fingers on my arms pulling me back to my desk, and her voice saying incomprehensible things to me in a hissing tone. Someone finally explained to her that I was new, that I did not speak English. I also remember how suddenly her face changed from anger to anxiety. But I did not forgive her for hitting me with that hard-cover spelling book. Yes, I would recognize that book even now. It was not until years later that I stopped hating that teacher for not understanding that I had been betrayed by a classmate, and by my inability to read her warning on the board. I instinctively understood then that language is the only weapon a child has against the absolute power of adults.

I quickly built up my arsenal of words by becoming an insatiable reader of books.

Schoolyard Magic

Leaning on the chainlink fence of P.S. No. 11,
my flesh cracking in the bitter breeze of a December day,
I burrow deep into my clothes and watch the black
   girls
jump rope so fast and hot my own skin responds.
Red, green, tartan coats balloon up around
long stem legs, making them exotic flowers and
   birds.
They sing a song to the beat of the slap-slap
of a clothesline on concrete:

   A sailor went to sea, sea, sea,
   To see what he could see, see, see,
   And all that he could see, see, see,
   Was the bottom of the deep, blue,
   Sea, sea, sea ...

The brick building framing their play,
the rusted fire-escape hanging over their heads,
the black smoke winding above in spirals,
all of it is wished away,
as I let my blood answer the summons of their song,
drawing my hands free from all my winter folds,
I clap until my palms turn red,
joining my voice to theirs,
rising higher than I ever dared.

El Olvido

It is a dangerous thing
to forget the climate of your birthplace
to choke out the voices of dead relatives
when in dreams they call you
by your secret name.
It is dangerous
to spurn the clothes you were born to wear
for the sake of fashion; dangerous
to use weapons and sharp instruments
you are not familiar with; dangerous
to disdain the plaster saints
before which your mother kneels
praying with embarrassing fervor
that you survive in the place you have chosen to
      live:
a bare, cold room with no pictures on the walls,
a forgetting place where she fears you will die
of loneliness and exposure.
Jesús, María y José, she says,
el olvido is a dangerous thing.

Tales Told Under the Mango Tree

María Sabida

Once upon a time there lived a girl who was so smart that she was known throughout Puerto Rico as María Sabida. María Sabida came into the world with her eyes open. They say that at the moment of her birth she spoke to the attending midwife and told her what herbs to use to make a special *guarapo*, a tea that would put her mother back on her feet immediately. They say that the two women would have thought the infant was possessed if María Sabida had not convinced them with her descriptions of life in heaven that she was touched by God and not spawned by the Devil.

María Sabida grew up in the days when the King of Spain owned Puerto Rico, but had forgotten to send law and justice to this little island lost on the map of the world. And so thieves and murderers roamed the land terrorizing the poor people. By the time María Sabida was of marriageable age, one such *ladrón* had taken over the district where she lived.

For years people had been subjected to abuse from this evil man and his henchmen. He robbed them of their cattle and then made them buy their own cows back from him. He would take their best chickens and produce when he came into town on Saturday afternoons riding with his men through the stalls set up by farmers. Overturning their tables, he would yell, "Put

69

it on my account." But of course he never paid for
anything he took. One year several little children disappeared while walking to the river, and although the
townspeople searched and searched, no trace of them
was ever found. That is when María Sabida entered
the picture. She was fifteen then, and a beautiful girl
with the courage of a man, they say.

She watched the chief *ladrón* the next time he ram-
paged through the pueblo. She saw that he was a young
man: red-skinned, and tough as leather. *Cuero y san-
gre, nada más*, she said to herself, a man of flesh and
blood. And so she prepared herself either to conquer or
to kill this man.

María Sabida followed the horses' trail deep into the
woods. Though she left the town far behind she never
felt afraid or lost. María Sabida could read the sun,
the moon, and the stars for direction. When she got
hungry, she knew which fruits were good to eat, which
roots and leaves were poisonous, and how to follow the
footprints of animals to a waterhole. At nightfall, María
Sabida came to the edge of a clearing where a large
house, almost like a fortress, stood in the forest.

"No woman has ever set foot in that house," she
thought, "no *casa* is this, but a man-place." It was
a house built for violence, with no windows on the
ground level, but there were turrets on the roof where
men could stand guard with guns. She waited until it
was nearly dark and approached the house through the
kitchen side. She found it by smell.

In the kitchen which she knew would have to have
a door or window for ventilation, she saw an old man
stirring a huge pot. Out of the pot stuck little arms and
legs. Angered by the sight, María Sabida entered the
kitchen, pushed the old man aside, and picking up the
pot threw its horrible contents out of the window.

"Witch, witch, what have you done with my master's stew!" yelled the old man. "He will kill us both when he gets home and finds his dinner spoiled."

"Get, you filthy *viejo*." María Sabida grabbed the old man's beard and pulled him to his feet. "Your master will have the best dinner of his life if you follow my instructions."

María Sabida then proceeded to make the most delicious *asopao* the old man had ever tasted, but she would answer no questions about herself, except to say that she was his master's fiancée.

When the meal was done, María Sabida stretched and yawned and said that she would go upstairs and rest until her *prometido* came home. Then she went upstairs and waited.

The men came home and ate ravenously of the food María Sabida had cooked. When the chief *ladrón* had praised the old man for a fine meal, the cook admitted that it had been *la prometida* who had made the tasty chicken stew.

"My what?" the leader roared, "I have no *prometida*." And he and his men ran upstairs. But there were many floors, and by the time they were halfway to the room where María Sabida waited, many of the men had dropped down unconscious and the others had slowed down to a crawl until they too were overcome with irresistible sleepiness. Only the chief *ladrón* made it to where María Sabida awaited him holding a paddle that she had found among his weapons. Fighting to keep his eyes open, he asked her, "Who are you, and why have you poisoned me?"

"I am your future wife, María Sabida, and you are not poisoned, I added a special sleeping powder that tastes like oregano to your *asopao*. You will not die."

"Witch!" yelled the chief *ladrón*, "I will kill you.

Don't you know who I am?" And reaching for her, he fell on his knees, whereupon María Sabida beat him with the paddle until he lay curled like a child on the floor. Each time he tried to attack her, she beat him some more. When she was satisfied that he was vanquished, María Sabida left the house and went back to town.

A week later, the chief *ladrón* rode into town with his men again. By then everyone knew what María Sabida had done and they were afraid of what these evil men would do in retribution. "Why did you not just kill him when you had a chance, *muchacha?*" many of the townswomen had asked María Sabida. But she had just answered mysteriously, "It is better to conquer than to kill." The townspeople then barricaded themselves behind closed doors when they heard the pounding of the thieves' horses approaching. But the gang did not stop until they arrived at María Sabida's house. There the men, instead of guns, brought out musical instruments: a *cuatro*, a *güiro*, *maracas*, and a harmonica. Then they played a lovely melody.

"María Sabida, María Sabida, my strong and wise María," called out the leader, sitting tall on his horse under María Sabida's window, "come out and listen to a song I've written for you—I call it *The Ballad of María Sabida.*"

María Sabida then appeared on her balcony wearing a wedding dress. The chief *ladrón* sang his song to her: a lively tune about a woman who had the courage of a man and the wisdom of a judge, and who had conquered the heart of the best *bandido* on the island of Puerto Rico. He had a strong voice and all the people cowering in their locked houses heard his tribute to María Sabida and crossed themselves at the miracle she had wrought.

One by one they all came out and soon María Sabida's front yard was full of people singing and dancing. The *ladrones* had come prepared with casks of wine, bottles of rum, and a wedding cake made by the old cook from the tender meat of coconuts. The leader of the thieves and María Sabida were married on that day. But all had not yet been settled between them. That evening, as she rode behind him on his horse, she felt the dagger concealed beneath his clothes. She knew then that she had not fully won the battle for this man's heart.

On her wedding night María Sabida suspected that her husband wanted to kill her. After their dinner, which the man had insisted on cooking himself, they went upstairs. María Sabida asked for a little time alone to prepare herself. He said he would take a walk but would return very soon. When she heard him leave the house, María Sabida went down to the kitchen and took several gallons of honey from the pantry. She went back to the bedroom and there she fashioned a life-sized doll out of her clothes and poured the honey into it. She then blew out the candle, covered the figure with a sheet and hid herself under the bed.

After a short time, she heard her husband climbing the stairs. He tip-toed into the dark room thinking her asleep in their marriage bed. Peeking out from under the bed, María Sabida saw the glint of the knife her husband pulled out from inside his shirt. Like a fierce panther he leapt onto the bed and stabbed the doll's body over and over with his dagger. Honey splattered his face and fell on his lips. Shocked, the man jumped off the bed and licked his lips.

"How sweet is my wife's blood. How sweet is María Sabida in death—how sour in life and how sweet in death. If I had known she was so sweet, I would not have murdered her." And so declaring, he kneeled down

on the floor beside the bed and prayed to María Sabida's
soul for forgiveness.

At that Moment María Sabida came out of her hid-
ing place. "Husband, I have tricked you once more, I
am not dead." In his joy, the man threw down his knife
and embraced María Sabida, swearing that he would
never kill or steal again. And he kept his word, becoming in later years an honest farmer. Many years later
he was elected mayor of the same town he had once
terrorized with his gang of *ladrones*.

María Sabida made a real *casa* out of his thieves'
den, and they had many children together, all of whom
could speak at birth. But, they say, María Sabida always
slept with one eye open, and that is why she lived to be
one hundred years old and wiser than any other woman
on the Island of Puerto Rico, and her name was known
even in Spain.

"Colorín, colorado este cuento se ha acabado." Mamá would slap her knees with open palms and say this
little rhyme to indicate to the children sitting around
her under the giant mango tree that the story was finished. It was time for us to go play and leave the women
alone to embroider in the shade of the tree and to talk
about serious things.

I remember that tree as a natural wonder. It was
large, with a trunk that took four or five children holding hands to reach across. Its leaves were so thick that
the shade it cast made a cool room where we took refuge
from the hot sun. When an unexpected shower caught
us there, the women had time to gather their embroi-
dery materials before drops came through the leaves.
But the most amazing thing about that tree was the
throne it had made for Mamá. On the trunk there was
a smooth seat-like projection. It was perfect for a story-
teller. She would take her place on the throne and lean

back. The other women—my mother and her sisters—
would bring towels to sit on; the children sat anywhere.
Sometimes we would climb to a thick branch we called
"the ship," to the right of the throne, and listen there.
"The ship" was a thick limb that hung all the way down
to the ground. Up to three small children could strad-
dle this branch while the others bounced on the end that
sat near the ground making it sway like a ship. When
Mamá told her stories, we sat quietly on our crow's nest
because if anyone interrupted her narrative she should
stop talking and no amount of begging would persuade
her to finish the story that day.

The first time my mother took my brother and me
back to Puerto Rico, we were stunned by the heat and
confused by a houseful of relatives. Mamá's *casa* was
filled to capacity with grandchildren, because two of the
married daughters had come to stay there until their
husbands sent for them: my mother and the two of us
and her oldest sister with her five children. Mamá still
had three of her own children at home, ranging in age
from a teenage daughter to my favorite uncle who was
six months older than me.

Our solitary life in New Jersey, where we spent our
days inside a small dark apartment watching television
and waiting for our father to come home on leave from
the navy, had not prepared us for life in Mamá's house
or for the multitude of cousins, aunts and uncles pulling
us into their loud conversations and rough games. For
the first few days my little brother kept his head firmly
buried in my mother's neck, while I stayed relatively
close to her; but being nearly six, and able to speak as
loudly as anyone, I soon joined Mamá's tribe.

In the last few weeks before the beginning of school,
when it was too hot for cooking until it was almost dark
and when mothers would not even let their boys go to

the playgrounds and parks for fear of sunstroke, Mamá would lead us to the mango tree, there to spin the web of her *cuentos* over us, making us forget the heat, the mosquitos, our past in a foreign country, and even the threat of the first day of school looming just ahead.

It was under that mango tree that I first began to feel the power of words. I cannot claim to have always understood the point of the stories I heard there. Some of these tales were based on ancient folklore brought to the colonies by Spaniards from their own versions of even older myths of Greek and Roman origins—which, as I later discovered through my insatiable reading— had been modified in clever ways to fit changing times. María Sabida became the model Mamá used for the "prevailing woman"—the woman who "slept with one eye open"—whose wisdom was gleaned through the senses: from the natural world and from ordinary experiences. Her main virtue was that she was always alert and never a victim. She was by implication contrasted to María La Loca, that poor girl who gave it all up for love, becoming a victim of her own foolish heart.

The mango tree was located at the top of a hill, on land that belonged to "The American," or at least to the sugar refinery that he managed. *La Central*, as it was called, employed the majority of the pueblo's men. Its tall chimney stacks loomed over the town like sentinels, spewing plumes of grey smoke that filled the air during cane season with the syrupy thick aroma of burnt sugar.

In my childhood the sugarcane fields bordered both sides of the main road, which was like a part on a head of spiky, green hair. As we approached the pueblo on our way coming home, I remember how my mother sat up in the back seat of the *carro público*, the taxi, we had taken from the airport in San Juan. Although she was pointing out the bell tower of the famous church of La Monserrate, I was distracted by the hypnotizing motion of men swinging machetes in the fields. They were shirtless, and sweat poured in streams down their backs. Bathed in light reflected by their blades, these laborers moved as on a ballet stage. I wondered whether they practiced like dancers to perfect their synchronicity. It did not occur to me that theirs was "survival choreography"—merely a safety measure—for wild swinging could lead to lost fingers and limbs. Or, as I heard one of the women say once, "there are enough body parts in the cane fields to put one whole man together."

And although trucks were already being used in most *centrales*, in our town, much of the cane harvest was still transported from the fields to the mill in oxen-drawn carts which were piled so high with the stalks, that, when you followed one of them you could see neither the cart driver nor the beasts in front: It was a moving haystack.

To car drivers they were a headache and a menace on the road. A good wind could blow the cane off the top of the cart and smash a windshield. But what most drivers hated was getting stuck behind one that would take up the whole road traveling at five miles per hour and ignore the horn, the mad hand waving and the red-faced man shouting invectives. In later years this vehicle would be almost totally replaced by the open-bed trucks that were also loaded to the limit, traveling the roads of the Island at sixty or seventy miles per hour, granting no other vehicle (except police cars) right-of-way. The driver would keep his hand on the horn and that was all the warning a passenger car received. Pulling over as if for an emergency vehicle was usually the best plan to follow.

We sucked on little pieces of sugar cane Mamá had

cut for us under the mango tree. Below us a pasture rolled down to the road and the cane fields could be seen at a distance; the men in their perpetual motion were tiny black ants to our eyes. You looked up to see the red roof of the American's house. It was a big white house with a large porch completely enclosed by mosquito screens (on the Island at that time this was such a rarity that all houses designed in that way were known as "American"). At Mamá's house we slept cozily under mosquito nets, but during the day we fought the stinging, buzzing insects with bare hands and, when we lost a battle, we soothed our scratched raw skin with calamine lotion.

During the first few weeks of our visits both my brother and I, because we were fresh, tender meat, had skin like a pink target, dotted with red spots where the insects had scored bulls-eyes. Amazingly, either we built up a natural resistance, or the mosquitoes gave up, but it happened every time: a period of embarrassment as pink "turistas," followed by brown skin and immunity. Living behind screens, the American couple would never develop the tough skin needed for Island survival.

When Mamá told stories about kings and queens and castles, she would point to the big house on the hill. We were not supposed to go near the place. In fact, we were trespassing when we went to the mango tree. Mamá's backyard ended at the barbed-wire fence that led to the American's pasture. The tree stood just on the other side. She had at some point before my time, placed a strong stick under the barbed wire to make an entrance; but it could only be pulled up so much, so that even the children had to crawl through. Mamá seemed to relish the difficulty of getting to our special place. For us children it was fun to watch our mothers get their hair and clothes caught on the wire and to listen to them curse.

The pasture was a magical realm of treasures and secret places to discover. It even had a forbidden castle we could look at from a distance.

While the women embroidered, my girl-cousins and I would gather leaves and thorns off a lemon tree and do some imaginative stitch work of our own. The boys would be in the "jungle" gathering banana leaves they built tepees with. Imitating the grownups who were never without a cigarette hanging from their mouths, we would pick the tightly wrapped buds of the hibiscus flowers, which, with their red tips, looked to us like lighted cigarettes. We glued wild flower petals to our fingernails and, although they did not stay on for long, for a little while our hands, busy puncturing the leaves into patterns with lemon tree thorns, looked like our mother's with their red nail polish, pushing needle and thread through white linen, creating improbable landscapes of trailing vines and flowers, decorating the sheets and pillowcases we would sleep on.

We picked ripe guavas in their season and dumped them on Mamá's capacious lap for her to inspect for worms before we ate them. The sweetness of a ripe guava cannot be compared to anything else: its pink, gooey inside can be held on the tongue and savored like a caramel.

During mango season we threw rocks at the branches of our tree, hanging low with fruit. Later in the season, a boy would climb to the highest branches for the best fruit—something I always yearned to do, but was not allowed to: too dangerous.

On days when Mamá felt truly festive she would send us to the store with three dollars for ten bottles of Old Colony pop and the change in assorted candies:

Mary Janes, Bazooka gum, lollypops, tiny two-piece boxes of Chicklets, coconut candy wrapped in wax paper, and more—all kept in big glass jars and sold two for one penny. We would have our reckless feast under the mango tree and then listen to a story. Afterwards, we would take turns on the swing that touched the sky.

My grandfather had made a strong swing from a plank of heavy wood and a thick length of rope. Under Mamá's supervision he had hung it from a sturdy lower branch of the mango tree that reached over the swell of the hill. In other words, you boarded the swing on level ground, but since the tree rose out of the summit, one push and you took off for the sky. It was almost like flying. From the highest point I ever reached, I could see the big house, as a bird would see it, to my left; the church tower from above the trees to my right; and far in the distance, below me, my family in a circle under the tree, receding, growing smaller; then, as I came back down to earth, looming larger, my mother's eyes glued to me, reflecting the fear for my safety that she would not voice in her mother's presence and thus risk overriding the other's authority. My mother's greatest fear was that my brother or I would hurt ourselves while at Mamá's, and that she would be held accountable by my excessively protective father when he returned from his tour of duty in Europe. And one day, because fear invites accident, I did fall from a ride up to the clouds.

I had been catapulting myself higher and higher, when out of the corner of my eye I saw my big cousin, Javier, running at top speed after his little brother, swinging a stick in front as if to strike the younger boy. This happened fast. The little boy, Roberto, ran towards Mamá, who at that moment, was leaning towards my mother in conversation. Trying to get to his brother before he reached safe haven, Javier struck, accidentally hitting my mother square on the face. I saw it happening. I saw it as if in slow motion. I saw my mother's broken glasses fly off her face, and the blood begin to flow. Dazed, I let go of the swing ropes and flew down from the clouds and the treetops and onto the soft cushion of pasture grass and just rolled and rolled. Then I lay there stunned, tasting grass and dirt until Mamá's strong arms lifted me up. She carried me through the fence and down to her house where my mother was calling hysterically for me. Her glasses had protected her from serious injury. The bump on her forehead was minor. The nosebleed had already been contained by the age-old method of placing a copper penny on the bridge, between the eyes. Her tears upset me, but not as much as the way she made me stand before her, in front of everyone, while she examined my entire body for bruises, scratches, and broken bones. "What will your father say," she kept repeating, until Mamá pulled me away. "Nothing," she said to my mother, "if you don't tell him." And, leaving her grown daughters to comfort each other, she called the children out to the yard where she had me organize a game of hide-and-seek that she supervised, catching cheaters right and left.

When it rained, the children were made to take naps or play quietly in the bedroom. I asked for Mamá's monumental poster bed, and, when my turn came, I got it. There I lay four or five feet above ground inhaling her particular smells of coconut oil, (which she used to condition her thick black hair) and Palmolive soap. I would luxuriate in her soft pillows and her mattress which was covered with gorgeously embroidered bed linens. I would get sleepy listening to the drone of the women's conversation out of the parlor.

Beyond the double doors of her peacock blue bedroom, I could hear Mamá and her older daughters talking about things that, at my age, would not have interested me: They read letters received from my father traveling with the navy in Europe, or letters from any of the many relatives making their way in the barrios of New York and New Jersey, working in factories and dreaming of returning "in style" to Puerto Rico.

The women would discuss the new school year, and plan a shopping trip to the nearest city, Mayagüez, for materials to make school uniforms for the children, who by September had to be outfitted in brown and white and marched off to the public school looking like Mussolini's troops in our dull uniforms. Their talk would take on more meaning for me as I got older, but that first year back on the Island I was under María Sabida's spell. To entertain myself, I would make up stories about the smartest girl in all of Puerto Rico.

When María Sabida was only six years old, I began, she saved her little brother's life. He was dying of a broken heart, you see, for he desperately wanted some sweet guavas that grew at the top of a steep, rocky hill near the lair of a fierce dragon. No one had ever dared to climb that hill, though everyone could see the huge guava tree and the fruit, as big as pears, hanging from its branches. María Sabida's little brother had stared at the tree until he had made himself sick from yearning for the forbidden fruit.

Everyone knew that the only way to save the boy was to give him one of the guavas. María Sabida's parents were frantic with worry. The little boy was fading fast. The father tried climbing the treacherous hill to the guava tree, but the rocks were loose and for every step forward he took, he slipped back three. He returned home. The mother spent her days cooking delicious meals with which to tempt her little son to eat, but he just turned his sad eyes to the window in his room from where he could see the guava tree loaded with the only food he wanted. The doctor came to examine the boy and pronounced him as good as gone. The priest came and told the women they should start making their black dresses. All hope seemed lost when María Sabida, whose existence everyone seemed to have forgotten, came up with an idea to save her brother one day while she was washing her hair in the special way her grandmother had taught her.

Her mamá had shown her how to collect rainwater— water from the sky—into a barrel, and then, when it was time to wash her hair, how to take a fresh coconut and draw the oil from its white insides. You then took a bowl of clear rainwater and added the coconut oil, using the mixture to rinse your hair. Her mamá had shown her how the rainwater, coming as it did from the sky, had little bits of starshine in it. This starstuff was what made your hair glossy, the oil was to make it stick.

It was while María Sabida was mixing the starshine that she had the brilliant idea which saved her brother. She ran to her father who was in the stable feeding the mule and asked if she could borrow the animal that night. The man, startled by his daughter's wild look (her hair was streaming wet and she still held the coconut scraps in her hands) at first just ordered his daughter into the house, thinking that she had gone crazy with grief over her brother's imminent death. But María Sabida could be stubborn, and she refused to move until her parents heard what she had to say. The man called his wife to the stable, and when María Sabida had finished telling them her plan, he still thought she had lost her mind. He agreed with his desperate wife that at this point anything was worth trying. They let María Sabida have the mule to use that night.

María Sabida then waited until it was pitch black. She knew there would be no moon that night. Then she drew water from her rainbarrel and mixed it with plenty of coconut oil and plastered her mule's hoofs with it. She led the animal to the bottom of the rocky hill where the thick, sweet smell of ripe guavas was irresistible. María Sabida felt herself caught in the spell. Her mouth watered and she felt drawn to the guava tree. The mule must have felt the same thing because it started walking ahead of the girl with quick, sure steps. Though rocks came tumbling down, the animal found footing, and in so doing, left a shiny path with the bits of starshine that María Sabida had glued to its hoofs. María Sabida kept her eyes on the bright trail because it was a dark, dark night.

As she approached the guava tree, the sweet aroma was like a liquid that she drank through her nose. She could see the fruit within arms-reach when the old mule stretched her neck to eat one and a horrible scaly arm reached out and yanked the animal off the path. María Sabida quickly grabbed three guavas and ran down the golden trail all the way back to her house.

When she came into her little brother's room, the women had already gathered around the bed with their flowers and their rosaries, and because María Sabida was a little girl herself and could not see past the crowd, she thought for one terrible minute that she was too late. Luckily, her brother smelled the guavas from just this side of death and he sat up in bed. María Sabida pushed her way through the crowd and gave him one to eat. Within minutes the color returned to his cheeks. Everyone rejoiced remembering other wonderful things that she had done, and why her middle name was "Sabida."

And, yes, María Sabida ate one of the enchanted guavas herself and was never sick a day in her long life.

The third guava was made into a jelly that could cure every childhood illness imaginable, from a toothache to the chicken pox.

"Colorín, colorado ... " I must have said to myself, "Colorín colorado ... " as I embroidered my own fable, listening all the while to that inner voice which, when I was very young, sounded just like Mamá's when she told her stories in the parlor or under the mango tree. And later, as I gained more confidence in my own ability, the voice telling the story became my own.

Fulana

She was the woman with no name. The blank
    filled in
with *Fulana* in the presence of children.
But we knew her—she was the wild girl
we were not allowed to play with,
who painted her face with her absent mother's
    make-up,
and who always wanted to be "wife"
when we played house. She was bored
with other games, preferred to turn the radio loud
to songs about women and men
loving and fighting to guitar, maracas, and drums.
She wanted to be a dancer on the stage,
dressed in nothing but yellow feathers.

And she would grow up careless as a bird,
losing contact with her name during the years
when her body was light enough to fly.
By the time gravity began to pull her down
to where the land animals chewed the cud
of domestic routine, she was a different
species. She had become *Fulana*, the creature
bearing the jagged scars of wings on her back,
whose name should not be mentioned
in the presence of impressionable little girls
who might begin to wonder about flight,
how the houses of their earth-bound mothers,
the fields and rivers, and the schools and churches
would look from above.

fulana nf (a) Doña F___ Mrs. So-and-so, Mrs. Blank, (b) (fam) tart (sl), whore.

Silent Dancing

We have a home movie of this party. Several times my mother and I have watched it together, and I have asked question about the silent revellers coming in and out of focus. It is grainy and of short duration but a great visual aid to my first memory of life in Paterson at that time. And it is in color—the only complete scene in color I can recall from those years.

We lived in Puerto Rico until my brother was born in 1954. Soon after, because of economic pressures on our growing family, my father joined the United States Navy. He was assigned to duty on a ship in Brooklyn Yard, New York City—a place of cement and steel that was to be his home base in the States until his retirement more than twenty years later.

He left the Island first, tracking down his uncle who lived with his family across the Hudson River, in Paterson, New Jersey. There he found a tiny apartment in a huge apartment building that had once housed Jewish families and was just being transformed into a tenement by Puerto Ricans overflowing from New York City. In 1955 he sent for us. My mother was only twenty years old, I was not quite three, and my brother was a toddler when we arrived at *El Building*, as the place had been christened by its new residents.

My memories of life in Paterson during those first few years are in shades of gray. Maybe I was too young

87

to absorb vivid colors and details, or to discriminate between the slate blue of the winter sky and the darker hues of the snow-bearing clouds, but the single color washes over the whole period. The building we lived in was gray, the streets were gray with slush the first few months of my life there, the coat my father had bought for me was dark in color and too big. It sat heavily on my thin frame.

I do remember the way the heater pipes banged and rattled, startling all of us out of sleep until we got so used to the sound that we automatically either shut it out or raised our voices above the racket. The hiss from the valve punctuated my sleep, which has always been fitful, like a nonhuman presence in the room—the dragon sleeping at the entrance of my childhood. But the pipes were a connection to all the other lives being lived around us. Having come from a house made for a single family back in Puerto Rico—my mother's extended-family home—it was curious to know that strangers lived under our floor and above our heads, and that the heater pipe went through everyone's apartments. (My first spanking in Paterson came as a result of playing tunes on the pipes in my room to see if there would be an answer). My mother was as new to this concept of beehive life as I was, but had been given strict orders by my father to keep the doors locked, the noise down, ourselves to ourselves.

It seems that Father had learned some painful lessons about prejudice while searching for an apartment in Paterson. Not until years later did I hear how much resistance he had encountered with landlords who were panicking at the influx of Latinos into a neighborhood that had been Jewish for a couple of generations. But it was the American phenomenon of ethnic turnover that was changing the urban core of Paterson, and the human flood could not be held back with an accusing finger.

"You Cuban?" the man had asked my father, pointing a finger at his name tag on the Navy uniform—even though my father had the fair skin and light brown hair of his northern Spanish family background and our name is as common in Puerto Rico as Johnson is in the U.S.

"No," my father had answered looking past the finger into his adversary's angry eyes "I'm Puerto Rican."

"Same shit." And the door closed. My father could have passed as European, but we couldn't. My brother and I both have our mother's black hair and olive skin, and so we lived in El Building and visited our great-uncle and his fair children on the next block. It was their private joke that they were the German branch of the family. Not many years later that area too would be mainly Puerto Rican. It was as if the heart of the city map were being gradually colored in brown—*café-con-leche* brown. Our color.

The movie opens with a sweep of the living room. It is "typical" immigrant Puerto Rican decor for the time: the sofa and chairs are square and hard-looking, upholstered in bright colors (blue and yellow in this instance, and covered in the transparent plastic) that furniture salesmen then were adept at making women buy. The linoleum on the floor is light blue, and if it was subjected to the spike heels as it was in most places, there were dime-sized identation all over it that cannot be seen in this movie. The room is full of people dressed in mainly two colors: dark suits for the men, red dresses for the women. I have asked my mother why most of the women are in red that night, and she shrugs, "I don't remember. Just a coincidence." She doesn't have my obsession for assigning symbolism to everything.

The three women in red sitting on the couch are my mother, my eighteen-year-old cousin, and her brother's girlfriend. The "novia" is just up from the Island, which is apparent in her body language. She sits up formally, and her dress is carefully pulled over her knees. She is a pretty girl but her posture makes her look insecure, lost in her full skirted red dress which she has carefully tucked around her to make room for my gorgeous cousin, her future sister-in-law. My cousin has grown up in Paterson and is in her last year of high school. She doesn't have a trace of what Puerto Ricans call "la mancha"(literally, the stain: the mark of the new immigrant—something about the posture, the voice, or the humble demeanor making it obvious to everyone that that person has just arrived on the mainland; has not yet acquired the pol-ished look of the city dweller). My cousin is wearing a tight red-sequined cocktail dress. Her brown hair has been lightened with peroxide around the bangs, and she is holding a cigarette very expertly between her fingers, bringing it up to her mouth in a sensuous arc of her arm to her as she talks animatedly with my mother, who has come to sit between the two women, both only a few years younger than herself. My mother is somewhere halfway between the poles they represent in our culture.

It became my father's obsession to get out of the ba-rrio, and thus we were never permitted to form bonds with the place or with the people who lived there. Yet the building was a comfort to my mother, who never got over yearning for *la isla*. She felt surrounded by her language: the walls were thin, and voices speaking and arguing in Spanish could be heard all day. *Salsas* blasted out of radios turned on early in the morning and left on for company. Women seemed to cook rice and beans perpetually—the strong aroma of red kidney beans boiling permeated the hallways.

Though Father preferred that we do our grocery shopping at the supermarket when he came home on weekend leaves, my mother insisted that she could cook only with products whose labels she could read, and so, during the week, I accompanied her and my little brother to *La Bodega*—a hole-in-the-wall grocery store across the street from *El Building*. There we squeezed down three narrow aisles jammed with various products. Goya and Libby's—those were the trademarks trusted by her Mamá, and so my mother bought cans of Goya beans, soups and condiments. She bought little cans of Libby's fruit juices for us. And she bought Colgate toothpaste and Palmolive soap. (The final *e* is pronounced in both those products in Spanish, and for many years I believed that they were manufactured on the Island. I remember my surprise at first hearing a commercial on television for the toothpaste in which Colgate rhymed with "ate.")

We would linger at La Bodega, for it was there that mother breathed best, taking in the familiar aromas of the foods she knew from Mamá's kitchen, and it was also there that she got to speak to the other women of El Building without violating outright Father's dictates against fraternizing with our neighbors.

But he did his best to make our "assimilation" painless. I can still see him carrying a Christmas tree up several flights of stairs to our apartment, leaving a trail of aromatic pine. He carried it formally, as if it were a flag in a parade. We were the only ones in El Building that I knew of who got presents on both Christmas Day and on *Día de Reyes*, the day when the Three Kings brought gifts to Christ and to Hispanic children.

Our greatest luxury in El Building was having our own television set. It must have been a result of Father's guilt feelings over the isolation he had imposed on us, but we were one of the first families in the barrio to have one. My brother quickly became an avid watcher of Captain Kangaroo and Jungle Jim. I loved all the family series, and by the time I started first grade in school, I could have drawn a map of Middle America as exemplified by the lives of characters in "Father Knows Best," "The Donna Reed Show," "Leave It to Beaver," "My Three Sons," and (my favorite) "Bachelor Father," where John Forsythe treated his adopted teenage daughter like a princess because he was rich and had a Chinese houseboy to do everything for him. Compared to our neighbors in El Building, we were rich. My father's Navy check provided us with financial security and a standard of life that the factory workers envied. The only thing his money could not buy us was a place to live away from the barrio—his greatest wish and Mother's greatest fear.

In the home movie the men are shown next, sitting around a card table set up in one corner of the living room, playing dominoes. The clack of the ivory pieces is a familiar sound. I heard it in many houses on the Island and in many apartments in Paterson. In "Leave It To Beaver," the Cleavers played bridge in every other episode; in my childhood, the men started every social occasion with a hotly debated round of dominoes: the women would sit around and watch, but they never participated in the games.

Here and there you can see a small child. Children were always brought to parties and, whenever they got sleepy, put to bed in the host's bedrooms. Babysitting was a concept unrecognized by the Puerto Rican women I knew: a responsible mother did not leave her children with any stranger. And in a culture where children are not considered intrusive, there is no need to leave the children at home. We went where our mother went.

Of my pre-school years I have only impressions: the sharp bite of the wind in December as we walked with our parents towards the brightly lit stores downtown, how I felt like a stuffed doll in my heavy coat, boots and mittens; how good it was to walk into the five-and-dime and sit at the counter drinking hot chocolate.

On Saturdays our whole family would walk downtown to shop at the big department stores on Broadway. Mother bought all our clothes at Penny's and Sears, and she liked to buy her dresses at the women's specialty shops like Lerner's and Diana's. At some point we would go into Woolworth's and sit at the soda fountain to eat.

We never ran into other Latinos at these stores or eating out, and it became clear to me only years later that the women from El Building shopped mainly at other places—stores owned either by other Puerto Ricans, or by Jewish merchants who had philosophically accepted our presence in the city and decided to make us their good customers, if not neighbors and friends. These establishments were located not downtown, but in the blocks around our street, and they were referred to generically as *La Tienda*, *El Bazar*, *La Bodega*, *La Botánica*. Everyone knew what was meant. These were the stores where your face did not turn a clerk to stone, where your money was as green as anyone else's.

On New Year's Eve we were dressed up like child models in the Sears catalogue—my brother in a miniature man's suit and bow tie, and I in a black patent leather shoes and a frilly dress with several layers of crinolines underneath. My mother wore a bright red dress that night, I remember, and spike heels; her long black hair hung to her waist. Father, who usually wore his Navy uniform during his short visits home, had put on a dark civilian suit for the occasion: we had been invited to his uncle's house for a big celebration. everyone was excited because my mother's brother, Hernán—a bachelor who could indulge himself in such luxuries—had bought a movie camera which he would be trying out that night.

Even the home movie cannot fill in the sensory details such a gathering left imprinted in a child's brain. The thick sweetness of women's perfume mixing with the ever-present smells of food cooking in the kitchen: meat and plantain *pasteles*, the ubiquitous rice dish made special with pigeon peas—*gandules*—and seasoned with the precious *sofrito* sent up from the island by somebody's mother or smuggled in by a recent traveler. *Sofrito* was one of the items that women hoarded, since it was hardly ever in stock at La Bodega. It was the flavor of Puerto Rico.

The men drank Palo Viejo rum and some of the younger ones got weepy. The first time I saw a grown man cry was at a New Year's Eve party. He had been reminded of his mother by the smells in the kitchen. But what I remember most were the boiled *pasteles*—boiled until the plantain or yucca rectangles stuffed with corned beef or other meats, olives, and many other savory ingredients, all wrapped in banana leaves. Everyone had to fish one out with a fork. There was always a "trick" pastel—one without stuffing—and whoever got that one was the "New Year's Fool."

There was also the music. Long-playing albums were treated like precious china in these homes. Mexican recordings were popular, but the songs that brought tears to my mother's eyes were sung by the melancholic Daniel Santos, whose life as a drug addict was the stuff of legend. Felipe Rodríguez was a particular favorite of couples. He sang about faithless women and broken-hearted men. There is a snatch of a lyric that has stuck

in my mind like a needle on a worn groove: "De piedra
ha de ser mi cama, de piedra la cabecera ... la mujer
que a mi me quiera ... ha de quererme de veras. Ay, Ay,
corazón, ¿por qué no amas ... ?" I must have heard it
a thousand times since the idea of a bed made of stone,
and its connection to love, first troubled me with its
disturbing images.

The five-minute home movie ends with people dancing in a circle. The creative filmmaker must have asked
them to do that so that they could file past him. It is
both comical and sad to watch silent dancing. Since
there is no justification for the absurd movements that
music provides for some of us, people appear frantic,
their faces embarrassingly intense. It's as if you were
watching sex. Yet for years, I've had dreams in the
form of this home movie. In a recurring scene, familiar faces push themselves forward into my mind's eye,
plastering their features into distorted close-ups. And
I'm asking them: "Who is she? Who is the woman I
don't recognize? Is she an aunt? Somebody's wife? Tell
me who she is. Tell me who these people are."

"No, see the beauty mark on her cheek as big as a
hill on the lunar landscape of her face—well, that runs
in the family. The women on your father's side of the
family wrinkle early; it's the price they pay for that fair
skin. The young girl with the green stain on her wedding
dress is *La Novia*—just up from the island. See, she
lowers her eyes as she approaches the camera like she's
supposed to. Decent girls never look you directly in the
face. *Humilde*, humble, a girl should express humility
in all her actions. She will make a good wife for your
cousin. He should consider himself lucky to have met
her only weeks after she arrived here. If he marries her
quickly, she will make him a good Puerto Rican-style
wife; but if he waits too long, she will be corrupted by

the city, just like your cousin there."

"She means me. I do what I want. This is not some primitive island I live on. Do they expect me to wear a black *mantilla* on my head and go to mass every day? Not me. I'm an American woman and I will do as I please. I can type faster than anyone in my senior class at Central High, and I'm going to be a secretary to a lawyer when I graduate. I can pass for an American girl anywhere—I've tried it—at least for Italian, anyway. I never speak Spanish in public. I hate these parties, but I wanted the dress. I look better than any of these *humildes* here. My life is going to be different. I have an American boyfriend. He is older and has a car. My parents don't know it, but I sneak out of the house late at night sometimes to be with him. If I marry him, even my name will be American. I hate rice and beans. It's what makes these women fat."

"Your *prima* is pregnant by that man she's been sneaking around with. Would I lie to you? I'm your great-uncle's common-law wife—the one he abandoned on the island to marry your cousin's mother. I was not invited to this party, but I came anyway. I came to tell you that story about your cousin that you've always wanted to hear. Remember that comment your mother made to a neighbor that has always haunted you? The only thing you heard was your cousin's name and then you saw your mother pick up your doll from the couch and say: 'It was as big as this doll when they flushed it down the toilet.' This image has bothered you for years, hasn't it? You had nightmares about babies being flushed down the toilet, and you wondered why anyone would do such a horrible thing. You didn't dare ask your mother about it. She would only tell you that you had not heard her right and yell at you for listening to adult conversations. But later, when

you were old enough to know about abortions, you suspected. I am here to tell you that you were right. Your
cousin was growing an *Americanito* in her belly when
this movie was made. Soon after she put something
long and pointy into her pretty self, thinking maybe she
could get rid of the problem before breakfast and still
make it to her first class at the high school. Well, *Niña*,
her screams could be heard downtown. Your aunt, her
Mamá, who had been a midwife on the Island, managed
to pull the little thing out. Yes, they probably flushed it
down the toilet, what else could they do with it—give
it a Christian burial in a little white casket with blue
bows and ribbons? Nobody wanted that baby—least
of all the father, a teacher at her school with a house in
West Paterson that he was filling with real children, and
a wife who was a natural blond.

Girl, the scandal sent your uncle back to the bottle.
And guess where you cousin ended up? Irony of ironies.
She was sent to a village in Puerto Rico to live with a
relative on her mother's side: a place so far away from
civilization that you have to ride a mule to reach it. A
real change in scenery. She found a man there. Women
like that cannot live without male company. But believe
me, the men in Puerto Rico know how to put a saddle
on a woman like her. *La Gringa*, they call her. ha, ha.
ha. *La Gringa* is what she always wanted to be ... "

The old woman's mouth becomes a cavernous black
hole I fall into. And as I fall, I can feel the reverber-
ations of her laughter. I hear the echoes of her last
mocking words: *La Gringa, La Gringa!* And the conga
line keeps moving silently past me. There is no music
in my dream for the dancers.

When Odysseus visits Hades asking to see the spirit
of his mother, he makes an offering of sacrificial blood,
but since all of the souls crave an audience with the

living, he has to listen to many of them before he can ask questions. I, too, have to hear the dead and the forgotten speak in my dream. Those who are still part of my life remain silent, going around and around in their dance. The others keep pressing their faces forward to say things about the past.

My father's uncle is last in line. He is dying of alcoholism, shrunken and shriveled like a monkey, his face is a mass of wrinkles and broken arteries. As he comes closer I realize that in his features I can see my whole family. If you were to stretch that rubbery flesh, you could find my father's face, and deep within *that* face—mine. I don't want to look into those eyes ringed in purple. In a few years he will retreat into silence, and take a long, long time to die. *Move back, Tío*, I tell him. *I don't want to hear what you have to say. Give the dancers room to move, soon it will be midnight. Who is the New Year's Fool this time?*

The Way My Mother Walked

She always wore an amulet on a gold chain,
an ebony fist
to protect her from the evil eye of envy
and the lust of men.
She was the gypsy queen of Market Street,
shuttling her caramel-candy body past
the blind window of the Jewish tailor
who did not lift his gaze,
the morse code of her stiletto heels sending
their Mayday-but-do-not-approach into
the darkened doorways where eyes
hung like mobiles in the breeze.
Alleys
Made her grasp my hand teaching me
the braille of her anxiety.
The two flights to our apartment were her holy
    ascension
to a sanctuary from strangers where evil
could not follow on its caterpillar feet and where
her needs and her fears could be put away
like matching towels on a shelf.

My Father in the Navy

Stiff and immaculate
in the white cloth of his uniform
and a round cap on his head like a halo,
he was an apparition on leave from a shadow-world
and only flesh and blood when he rose from below
the waterline where he kept watch over the engines
and dials making sure the ship parted the waters
on a straight course.
Mother, brother and I kept vigil
on the nights and dawns of his arrival,
watching the corner beyond the neon sign of a
    quasar
for the flash of white, our father like an angel
heralding a new day.
His homecomings were the verses
we composed over the years making up
the siren's song that kept him coming back
from the bellies of iron whales
and into our nights
like the evening prayer.

Some of the Characters

Vida

To a child, life is a play directed by parents, teachers, and other adults who are forever giving directions: "Say this," "Don't say that," "Stand here," "Walk this way," "Wear these clothes," and on and on and on. If we miss or ignore a cue, we are punished. And so we memorized the script of our lives as interpreted by our progenitors, and we learned not to extemporize too much: the world—our audience—likes the well-made play, with everyone in their places and not too many bursts of brilliance or surprises. But once in a while new characters walk onto the stage, and the writers have to scramble to fit them in, and for a while, life gets interesting.

Vida was a beautiful Chilean girl who simply appeared in the apartment upstairs with her refugee family one day and introduced herself into our daily drama.

She was tall, thin and graceful as a ballerina, with fair skin and short black hair. She looked like a gazelle as she bounded down the stairs from her apartment to ours the day she first came to our door to borrow something. Her accent charmed us. She said that she had just arrived from Chile with her sister, her sister's newborn baby girl, her sister's husband, and their grandmother. They were all living together in a one-bedroom apartment on the floor above us.

There must have been an interesting story of political exile there, but I was too young to care about that
detail. I was immediately fascinated by the lovely Vida
who looked like one of the models in the fashion magazines that I, just turning twelve, had begun to be interested in. Vida came into my life during one of my
father's long absences with the Navy, so that his constant vigilance was not a hindrance to my developing
attachment to this vibrant human being. It was not a
friendship—she was too much older than I and too self-
involved to give me much in return for my devotion.
It was more a Sancho Panza/Knight of La Mancha relationship, with me following her while she explored the
power of her youth and beauty.

Vida wanted to be a movie star in Hollywood. That
is why she had come to America, she said. I believed
that she would be, although she spoke almost no English. That was my job, she said, to teach her to speak
perfect English without an accent. She had finished sec-
ondary school in her country, and although she was only
sixteen, she was not going to school in Paterson. She
had other plans. She would get a job as soon as she
had papers, save money, then she would leave for Hollywood as soon as possible. She asked me how far Hollywood was. I showed her the state of California in
my geography book. She traced a line with her finger
from New Jersey to the west coast and smiled. Nothing
seemed impossible to Vida.

It was summer when I met Vida, and we spent our
days in the small, fenced-in square lot behind our apartment building, avoiding going indoors as much as possible, since it was depressing to Vida to hear her family talking about the need to find jobs; to smell sour
baby smells, or to be constantly lectured to by her obese
grandmother who sat like a great pile of laundry on a

couch all day, watching shows on television which she did not understand. The brother-in-law frightened me a little with his intense eyes and his constant pacing. He spoke in whispers to his wife, Vida's sister, when I was around, as if he did not want me to overhear important matters, making me feel like an intruder. I didn't like to look at Vida's sister. She looked like a Vida who had been left out in the elements for too long: skin stuck to the bones. Vida did not like her family either. When I asked, she said that her mother was dead and that she did not want to speak of the past. Vida thought only of the future.

Once, when we were alone in her apartment, she asked me if I wanted to see her in a bathing suit. She went into the bathroom and emerged in a tight red one-piece suit. She reclined on the bed in a pose she had obviously seen in a magazine. "Do you think I am beautiful?" she asked me. I answered yes, suddenly overwhelmed by a feeling of hopelessness for my skinny body, bony arms and legs, flat chest. "Cadaverous," Vida had once whispered, smiling wickedly into my face after taking my head into her hands and feeling my skull so close to the surface. But right afterwards she had kissed my cheek reassuring me that I would "flesh out" in a few years.

That summer my life shifted on its axis. Until Vida, my mother had been the magnetic force around which all my actions revolved. Since my father was away for long periods of time, my young mother and I had developed a strong symbiotic relationship, with me playing the part of interpreter and buffer to the world for her. I knew at an early age that I would be the one to face landlords, doctors, store clerks, and other "strangers" whose services we needed in my father's absence. English was my weapon and my power. As long as she lived in her fantasy that her exile from Puerto Rico was temporary and that she did not need to learn the language, keeping herself "pure" for her return to the Island, then I was in control of our lives outside the realm of our little apartment in Paterson—that is, until Father came home from his Navy tours: then the mantle of responsibility would fall on him. At times, I resented his homecomings, when I would suddenly be thrust back into the role of dependent which I had long ago outgrown—and not by choice.

But Vida changed me. I became secretive, and every outing from our apartment building—to get my mother a pack of L&M's; to buy essentials at the drugstore or supermarket (which my mother liked to do on an as-needed basis); and, Vida's favorite, to buy Puerto Rican groceries at the *bodega*—became an adventure with Vida. She was getting restless living in such close quarters with her paranoid sister and brother-in-law. The baby's crying and the pervasive smells of dirty diapers drove her crazy as well as her fat grandmother's lethargy disturbed only by the old woman's need to lecture Vida about her style of dress and her manners, which even my mother had started to comment on.

Vida was modeling herself on the Go-Go girls she loved to watch on dance shows on our television set. She would imitate their movements with me as her audience until we both fell on the sofa laughing. Her eye make-up (bought with my allowance) was dark and heavy, her lips were glossy with iridescent tan lipstick, and her skirts were riding higher and higher on her long legs. When we walked up the street on one of my errands, the men stared; the Puerto Rican men did more than that. More than once we were followed by men inspired to compose *piropos* for Vida—erotically charged words spoken behind us in stage whispers.

I was scared and excited by the trail of Vida's admirers. It was a dangerous game for both of us, but for me especially, since my father could come home unannounced at any time and catch me at it. I was the invisible partner in Vida's life; I was the little pocket mirror she could take out any time to confirm her beauty and her power. But I was too young to think in those terms, all I knew was the thrill of being in her company, being touched by her magical powers of transformation that could make a walk to the store a deliciously sinful escapade.

Then Vida fell in love. He was, in my jealous eyes, a Neanderthal, a big hairy man who drove a large black Oldsmobile recklessly around our block hour after hour just to catch a glimpse of Vida. He had promised to drive her to California, she confided to me. Then she started to use me as cover in order to meet him, asking me to take a walk with her, then leaving me to wait on a park bench or at the library for what seemed an eternity while she drove around with her muscle-bound lover. I became disenchanted with Vida, but remained loyal to her throughout the summer. Once in a while we still shared a good time. She loved to tell me in detail about her "romance." Apparently, she was not totally naive, and had managed to keep their passionate encounters within the limits of kissing and petting in the spacious backseat of the black Oldsmobile. But he was getting impatient, she told me, so she had decided to announce her engagement to her family soon. They would get married and go to California together. He would be her manager and protect her from the Hollywood "wolves."

By this time I was getting weary of Vida's illusions about Hollywood. I was glad when school started in the fall and I got into my starched blue jumper only to discover that it was too tight and too short for me. I had "developed" over the summer.

Life settled to our normal routine when we were in the States. This was: my brother and I went to Catholic school and did our lessons, our mother waited for our father to come home on leave from his Navy tours, and all of us waited to hear when we would be returning to Puerto Rico—which was usually every time Father went to Europe, every six months or so. Vida would sometimes come down to our apartment and complain bitterly about life with her family upstairs. They had absolutely refused to accept her fiancé. They were making plans to migrate elsewhere. She did not have work papers yet, but did not want to go with them. She would have to find a place to stay until she got married. She began courting my mother. I would come home to find them looking at bride magazines and laughing together. Vida hardly spoke to me at all.

Father came home in his winter blues and everything changed for us. I felt the almost physical release of the burden of responsibility for my family and allowed myself to spend more time doing what I like to do best of all—read. It was a solitary life we led in Paterson, New Jersey, and both my brother and I became avid readers. My mother did too, although because she had little English, her fare was made up of *Corín Tellado* romances, which the drugstore carried, and the *Buenhogar* and *Vanidades* magazines that she received in the mail occasionally. But she read less and I more when Father came home. The ebb and flow of this routine was interrupted by Vida that year. With my mother's help she introduced herself into our family.

Father, normally a reticent man, suspicious of strangers by nature, and always vigilant about dangers to his children, also fell under Vida's spell. Amazingly, he agreed to let her come stay in our apartment until her wedding some months away. She moved into my room. She slept on what had been my little brother's twin bed until he got his own room, a place where I liked to keep my collection of dolls from around the world that my father had sent me. These had to be put in a box in the dark closet now.

Vida's perfume took over my room. As soon as I walked in, I smelled her. It got on my clothes. The nuns at my school commented on it since we were not allowed to use perfume or cosmetics. I tried to wash it off, but it was strong and pervasive. Vida tried to win me over by taking me shopping. She was getting money from her boyfriend—for her trousseau—she said. She bought me a tight black skirt just like hers and a pair of shoes with heels. When she had me model it for my family, my father frowned and left the room silently. I was not allowed to keep the things. Since the man was never seen at our house, we did not know that Vida had broken the engagement and was seeing other men.

My mother started to complain about little things Vida did, or did not do. She did not help with house-work, although she did contribute money. Where was she getting it? She did not bathe daily (a major in-fraction in my mother's eyes), but poured cologne over herself in quantities. She claimed to be at church too many times a week and came home smelling of alcohol, even though it was hard to tell because of the perfume. Mother was spreading her wings and getting ready to fight for exclusivity over her nest.

But, Father, surprising us all again, argued for fair-ness for the *señorita*—my mother made a funny "har-rump" noise at that word, which in Spanish connotes virginity and purity. He said we had promised her asy-lum until she got settled and it was important that we send her out of our house in a respectable manner: married, if possible. He liked playing cards with her. She was cunning and smart, a worthy adversary.

Mother fumed. My brother and I spent a lot of time in the kitchen or living room, reading where the air was not saturated with "Evening in Paris."

Vida was changing. After a few months, she no longer spoke of Hollywood; she barely spoke to me at all. She got her papers and got a job in a factory sewing dungarees. Then, almost as suddenly as she had come into my life, she disappeared.

One afternoon I came home to find my mother mopping the floors strenuously with a pine cleaner, giving the apartment the kind of thorough scrubbing usually done as a family effort in the spring. When I went into my room the dolls were back in their former place on the extra bed. No sign of Vida.

I don't remember discussing her parting much. Although my parents were fair, they did not always feel the need to explain or justify their decisions to us. I have always believed that my mother simply demanded her territory, fearing the growing threat of Vida's beauty and erotic slovenliness that was permeating her clean home. Or perhaps Vida found life with us as stifling as she had with her family. If I had been a little older, I would have learned more from Vida, but she came at a time when I needed security more than knowledge of human nature. She was a fascinating creature.

The last time I saw Vida's face it was on a poster. It announced her crowning as a beauty queen for a Catholic church in another parish. Beauty contests were held by churches as fundraisers at that time, as contradictory as that seems to me now: a church sponsoring a competition to choose the most physically attractive female in the congregation. I still feel that it was right to see Vida wearing the little tiara of fake diamonds in that photograph with the caption underneath: *Vida wins!*

San Antonio al Revés

You are the patron saint
of women who wait
lighting candles at your feet,
San Antonio,
every Saturday morning and night,
that you intercede
for them in God's blue heaven
and save their sons and husbands
from the rum-slick bodies of *putas*,
and deliver them
from the blades of drunken friends.
Virgins
stand you on your blessed head,
San Antonio al revés,
for luck, promising hymns
as dowry, and their prayers
are like an extra blanket
at the foot of their winter beds,
San Antonio, San Antonio al revés.

Providencia

Inevitably we all lose our innocence about the basic fact that life begins with the most biologically basic act, that the mystery of birth does not require esoteric knowledge or magical powers. But there is a little bit of time when, as we are poised to receive this "terrible burden," we can still be awed by the miracle of babies. As a young girl, sheltered by my parents and kept away from forbidden knowledge by the nuns who taught me, and the well meaning librarian who limited my access to books, I was willing to believe for a while that babies came from the seventh floor of our apartment building in Paterson, New Jersey. That is where the fertile Providencia lived with her ever growing tribe of brown cherubs.

My memory of Providencia is strictly visual. I never spoke to her. My mother would not have allowed it. Providencia was the whispered joke told by women in their kitchens, she was the social worker's nightmare and a walking threat to the ideals of marriage and fidelity. Her children were an accumulation rather than a family. No one was sure who the fathers were. Although they speculated, they also avoided close inspection, because it could have been dangerous to ask too many questions—our neighborhood was not so large that Providencia's promiscuity could avoid being a matter of personal concern to the wives and mothers.

She seemed to be always pregnant. I see her as a pleasant looking brown-skinned woman with a roundness to her figure that was classical—like a Hispanic model for Reubens. She was fleshy, slow moving, both ultimately maternal and sensuous—the Magna Mate

She seemed content, although her life must have been very difficult. The children (I never knew exactly how many) did not appear neglected, and there was a raggedy troupe aspect to them. They wore each others' hand-me-downs, but were noisy and playful. I would see them at the public park where Providencia took them occasionally—a place I could only pass by because my brother and I had been forbidden to go there alone. My mother called it "el parque de los bums," the bums' park, since it had been taken over by homeless men who constructed their cardboard shelters over the playground equipment at night and slept on the benches during the day. The police chased them out regularly, but with the persistence of the dispossessed, they always returned. Providencia sat among them wearing a calm madonna smile and watching her children play. She seemed unaffected by the human degradation around her. Perhaps she was truly possessed of spiritual calm; her face usually wore the beatific smile I was used to seeing on the visage of Mary and other female saints in religious paintings: St. Agnes on her decapitation block smiled like that; St. Theresa in her prayerful ecstasy; and of course, the Madonna holding her Child. More likely, though, Providencia was disconnected from reality. In a setting different from a Puerto Rican barrio, where her behavior might have been labeled by both her peers and the authorities with moralistic and sociological tags, she would have been recognized as a damaged personality and treated clinically.

As it was, the woman was a burden to society, but not a major problem in an immigrant neighborhood where the subtleties of mental illness may become buried in the larger preoccupation with "la lucha"—the daily struggle.

And so Providencia entertained men in her apartment paid for by the state, and she had babies, to be fed and clothed by the state. I listened to the women talk about this "desgraciada"—the woman who brings shame—and I heard the resentment and the fear in their voices and so learned that a woman's body, with its capabilities to produce new lives, is a trump card in the balance of human relationships. And Providencia was like an "idiot savant" in a game of chance that these women tried to control very carefully; Providencia's careless bets made them very nervous, for to her losing meant winning. She simply did not care about the rules.

Why Providencia Has Babies

No husband, but many men
climbed the steps to Providencia's place;
a loft in an old building, filled with children
hanging from her skirts, one at her breast,
and another always on the way.
She was the welfare madonna on our block,
and the women's joke
I didn't get for many years.

I heard that as a young girl
Providencia had been left alone
in dark, unheated rooms while her mother
worked the streets. I imagine her loneliness,
tangible as breath on a cold night,
and how she talked to the shadows
moved by streetlights. Perhaps the first
time was a result of violence,
and as she listened to her body's new pulse
she felt less alone; maybe she dreamed
a visitation for herself:
the flutter of wings she heard
was not just city-grayed pigeons
at the window ledge,
and the voice in the hall saying,
Ave María, was more
than a tired old woman's complaint
at the top of a punishing staircase—

it was an absolution.
                    When Providencia
first felt the stirrings of life deep inside—
below the ribcage, under the heart,
where a woman's soul nests—her life was resolved.
She learned a lesson she would never forget:
that as long as she lived,
she need never be lonely again.

Salvatore

Sal was the super in one of the apartment buildings
where we lived. He was Italian and he was homosexual.
The word "gay" was not in use then, and the concept
of homosexuality was so mysterious and frightening to
most of the people I knew as a child that the only ref-
erences I heard to it were derisive or humorous, that is,
when it was referred to at all. When speaking of Sal, for
example, someone would usually make the gesture of a
limp wrist. I laughed along with the others, not knowing anything beyond the fact that Sal was very different
from my father and the other men and boys I knew. For
one thing, Sal liked to cook.

We lived in Sal's building during the Cuban missile crisis. Somewhere on a ship in the Caribbean, my
father was not allowed to communicate with us for several months. It was a very difficult time for my mother
who was used to receiving directions from him by mail.
During his long absences, he sent us back to Puerto Rico
to stay with her mother. Our lives thus followed a certain erratic pattern decided by his travels. But this time
there was radio silence. We were on our own. And if
Sal had not hovered over us as if we were his brood, it
would have been an even more traumatic time for my
young mother, my brother and myself.

It was not as if he solved our troubles. Sal had
a strict "hands-off" policy about his tenants' personal
problems. If the rent was late, anyone living there would
find a note taped to the door. Two warnings, and you
were out. Sal's kindness had more to do with his intense need to nurture. In us he found the acceptance
for his ministerings—the absence of suspicion—that he
needed to inspire him into fabulous culinary feats which
he brought to our door in steaming pans: lasagna done
from scratch with the most delicate cheeses, spaghetti

topped with creative sauces, Italian pastries, and more. He filled our little apartment with the comforting aromas of meals cooked with caring, while we waited for our future to become clear again.

His private life was a mystery to us. We were never invited to his first floor apartment. But a glimpse of his elaborate taste could be gotten from the artfully draped curtains and the hanging plants at his window. In a little square of real earth in what was idealistically called a "backyard" in the urban core of Paterson—a fenced off area where the garbage bins were located—Sal had incredibly created a real vegetable garden. Each spring he would turn the earth, adding rich black soil to it and begin the ceaseless tending again. I would sometimes sit on the bottom step and watch him: a slight man, with large peasant features, gray hair cut very close to the skull. He would be wearing chinos and a sports shirt with the collar turned up, a large apron with many pockets for his tools, rubber gloves, and my favorite—a big straw hat. The gardening scene was in such contrast to the traffic, cement, and crowds on the other side of the building that it fascinated me. My brother and I often talked about how a swimming pool would fit nicely right where Sal planted, and if not a pool, then a swing set. But those were our "suburban" fantasies. The only children we knew who lived in single houses with backyard equipment were on television or in Puerto Rico. Paterson to us meant indoor activities.

Sal grew tiny tomatoes, round and perfect as Christmas balls. And he grew zucchini with shiny green skin, and lettuce which sprang out of the soil like a Martian rose. He would place the vegetables lovingly into a straw basket and bring some to my mother who would coo over them as if they were a baby, but later throw them out, since they were "Italian" ingredients that could not be made into anything Puerto Rican in her kitchen.

Sal kept his hands busy all day but he acted like a lonely man. He could not have had friendships with the men in our building for whom he was an object of derision. Even my father chose to avoid contact with Sal, letting my mother go to the door when we heard Sal's familiar padding footsteps approaching. He was accorded "special" treatment by the women too. They would say and do things around him that they would never do in front of "real" men, such as discussing intimate matters and trying to draw him into gossip and sexual innuendo.

In thinking back, the closest I ever came to understanding the pathos of Sal's life was the time when my wild and romantic uncle Hernán came to visit us in Paterson. My mother's younger brother, the "black sheep" of her family, arrived at our door without warning after one of his many misadventures; broke, unemployed, and charming, he came seeking "asylum" at his sister's house. My brother and I fell totally under the spell of this dark, energetic, unpredictable man; the complete opposite of our soft-spoken father. Hernán filled the house with the electricity of his personality. We begged our mother to let him stay, despite our apartment being too small even for the three of us. But, I argued, that with Father away at present, she could sleep with me and Hernán could have their bed. She too was at first charmed by her brother's new worldliness, and his presence would be a balm for her constant homesickness, but her hesitation had nothing to do with lack of space; having shared a house with eight brothers and sisters in Puerto Rico had made my mother indifferent to the usual concerns about room and privacy that we felt. Her reticence had to do with Sal's strict rule about guests.

When we had moved from the place that Paterson's Puerto Ricans called "El Building," Father had warned us that in a mixed neighborhood there would be rules to follow. It was a "step up" from the barrio, and we were expected to behave with restraint, he had explained, to defeat the stereotype of the loud, slovenly tenement-dweller. He had agreed to Sal's rules for his tenants—no long-term guests was one of them. Mother told us about this agreement as we sat at the kitchen table considering how to keep our uncle with us. It was then that Sal came to the door with a steaming plate of vegetables. And Hernán went into action.

As soon as Sal saw the curly haired, wiry Hernán, he was transformed. He became very talkative, asking Mother to introduce him and going as far as joining us at the table, something he had never done before. Soon, we were completely left out of the conversation. I noticed that Hernán was laughing a lot, showing his strong white teeth on that Indian face of his, and I remember feeling jealous for his attention. But, being a child, I must have turned to something else. All I know was that when Sal left, Hernán moved in, much to our delight. And almost every day during the few weeks of his visit, Sal would predictably show up at our door with one excuse or another. His eyes would be bright and his face rosy—as if he had just shaved and scrubbed. For a while Hernán played the game. Afterwards Hernán and Mother would sit at the table smoking their L&M's and drinking coffee. They would joke about Sal's visits and laugh over the things that he said to Hernán. Their favorite was Sal's comment about Hernán being such a handsome "brunet."

Hernán's visit meant for my brother and me a reprieve from the constant concern over Father. He made the rounds with us to the Red Cross, to the Veterans' Administration, to endless offices where we were trying to get answers about Father's whereabouts. Hernán charmed secretaries and got us appointments; and mainly he helped us pass the time while we waited and waited to hear something other than the official statement that the ship's location was classified until the Cuban "situation" was resolved.

But as soon as Hernán found a job, in some factory in Clifton, and made new friends, he changed. His "wild" side, often talked about by my mother, started becoming evident. He came home late, waking us as he drunkenly burst through the door. He spent all his money on heavily wagered dominoes and card games—which were dutifully reported to Mother by women in the neighborhood whose husbands had the same vices. And he began smoking what we were told by Mother—who found them in his pockets when she did his laundry—were "funny cigarettes." She felt that he should find a place of his own, but was having difficulty telling him. And there was Sal with his melancholy eyes at the door every day asking about Hernán.

The stabbing incident ended our romance with our incorrigible relative. I did not get all the facts until much later, but apparently Hernán had been seeing a married woman whose husband showed up without warning. The result was a knife wound, sort of like the mark of Zorro scratched across my uncle's back as he fled the scene. He was taken to the hospital by friends who came in the middle of the night to tell my mother. She suffered intensely from the gossip and humiliation, and the next time we saw Hernán, a little more subdued but unrepentant, he had moved into a boarding house.

Sal must have heard the story too, and he stayed away from our apartment. He worked with unparalleled frenzy in his garden, but did not share his bountiful harvest with us that season. That year our father returned to us a changed man too. The six months isolated on a ship circling Cuba—unable to communicate with us, frightened for our lives and for the world—had locked him inside himself. He had grown old. And I too had changed while waiting to know about my father, listening to the President speak about the "threat to the free world" from the grainy screen of our T.V.; pleading with strangers to listen to me, a skinny Puerto Rican child; taking my mother from office to office: "Where is my father, her husband? Where is he?" But when he was returned to us he was a different man, and I did not recognize the sullen stranger as my quiet but tender *Papi*. The end of childhood had arrived like a black-bordered telegram delivered in silence to the door.

Sal, we are as alone as you: Locked inside the bodies of strangers, unable to touch the ones we love most.

En Mis Ojos No Hay Días

Back before the fire burned behind his eyes,
in the blast furnace which finally consumed him,
Father told us about the reign of little terrors
of his childhood, beginning
at birth with his father who cursed him
for being the twelfth and the fairest,
too blond and pretty to be from his loins,
so he named him the priest's pauper son.
Father said the old man kept
a mule for labor
wine in his cellar
a horse for sport
a mistress in town
and a wife to bear him daughters,
to send to church
to pray for his soul,
and sons,
to send to the fields
to cut the cane
and raise the money
to buy his rum.
He was only ten when he saw his father
split a man in two with his machete
and walk away proud to have rescued his honor
like a true "hombre."
Father always wrapped these tales
in the tissue paper of his humor
and we'd listen at his knee,
rapt, warm and safe
in the blanket of his caring.

But he himself could not be saved.
To this day his friends still ask,
"What on earth drove him mad?"
Remembering Prince Hamlet I reply,
"Nothing on earth,"
but no one listens to ghost stories anymore.

The Looking-Glass Shame

> "At any rate, the looking-glass shame has lasted all my life."
>
> —Virginia Woolf, *Moments of Being*

In her memoir, *Moments of Being*, Virginia Woolf tells of a frightening dream she had as a young girl in which, as she looked at herself in the mirror, she saw something moving in the background: " ... a horrible face—the face of an animal ... " over her shoulder. She never forgot that "other face in the glass" perhaps because it was both alien and familiar. It is not unusual for an adolescent to feel disconnected from her body—a stranger to herself and to her new developing needs—but I think that to a person living simultaneously in two cultures this phenomenon is intensified.

Even as I dealt with the trauma of leaving childhood, I saw that "cultural schizophrenia" was undoing many others around me at different stages of their lives. Society gives clues and provides rituals for the adolescent but withholds support. As I entered my freshman year of high school in a parochial school, I was given a new uniform to wear: a skirt and blouse as opposed to the severe blue jumper with straps, to accommodate for developing breasts, I suppose, although I would have little to accommodate for an excruciatingly long time—being a "skinny bones," as my classmates often called me, with no hips or breasts to speak of. But the warnings began, nevertheless. At home my mother constantly reminded me that I was now a "señorita" and needed to behave accordingly; but she never explained exactly what that entailed. She had said the same thing when I had started menstruating a couple of years before. At school the classrooms and the cafeteria were segregated into "boyside" and "girlside." The nuns kept a hawk-eye on the length of the girls' skirts, which had to come to below the knee at a time when the mini-skirt was becoming the micro-skirt out in the streets.

After school, I would see several of the "popular" girls walk down to the corner out of sight from the school, and get into cars with public school boys. Many of the others went down to the drugstore to have a soda and talk loudly and irreverently about the school and the nuns. Most of them were middle class Italian and Irish kids. I was the only Puerto Rican student, having gotten in after taking a rigorous academic test and after the priest visited our apartment to ascertain that we were a good Catholic family. I felt lost in the sea of bright white faces and teased blond hair of the girls who were not unkind to me, but did not, at least that crucial first year, include me in their groups that traveled together to skating rinks, basketball games, pizza parlors—those activities that they would talk about on Monday in their rapid-fire English as we all awaited to be let into the building.

Not that I would have been allowed to go to these places. I lived in the carefully constructed facsimile of a Puerto Rican home my mother had created. Every day I crossed the border of two countries: I would spend the day in the pine-scented parochial school building where exquisitely proper behavior was the rule strictly enforced by the soft spoken nuns, who could, upon observing an infraction of their many rules, turn into despots—and never raise their voices—as they destroyed your peace of mind with threats of shameful exposure and/or expulsion. But there was order, quiet, respect for logic, and there, also, I received the information I was always hungry for. I liked reading books, and I took immense pleasure in the praise of the teachers for my attentiveness and my good grades. So what, I thought to myself, if I was not invited to the homes of my classmates who did not live in my neighborhood, anyway. I lived in the city core, in an apartment that may have housed an Italian or Irish family a generation before. Now they were prosperous and had moved to the suburbs and the Puerto Ricans had moved into the "immigrant" apartment buildings. That year I actually felt a sense of burning shame at the fact that I did not have to take a bus or be picked up in a car to go home. I lived only a few blocks away from the church and the school which had been built in the heart of the city by the original wave of Irish Catholics—for *their* convenience. The Puerto Ricans had built no churches.

I would walk home every day from school. I had fifteen minutes to get home before my mother panicked and came after me. I did not want that to happen. She was so different from my classmates' mothers that I was embarrassed to be seen with her. While most of the other mothers were stoutly built women with dignified grey hair who exuded motherliness, my mother was an exotic young beauty, black hair down to her waist and a propensity for wearing bright colors and spike heels. I would have died of shame if one of my classmates had seen her sensuous walk and the looks she elicited from the men on our block. And she would have embraced me in public, too, for she never learned moderation in her emotions, or restraint for her gesturing hands and loud laughter. She kept herself a "native" in that apartment she rarely left, except on my father's arm, or to get one of us from school. I had had to have a shouting match with her to convince her that I no longer needed to be escorted back and forth from school in the ninth grade.

My mother carried the island of Puerto Rico over her head like the mantilla she wore to church on Sunday. She was "doing time" in the U.S. She did not know how long her sentence would last, or why she was being punished with exile, but she was only doing it for her children. She kept herself "pure" for her eventual return to the island by denying herself a social life (which would have connected her too much with the place); by never learning but the most basic survival English; and by her ability to create an environment in our home that was a comfort to her, but a shock to my senses, and I suppose, to my younger brother's, both of us having to enter and exit this twilight zone of sights and smells that meant *casa* to her.

In our apartment we spoke Spanish, we ate rice and beans with meats prepared in *adobo*, that mouth-watering mixture of spices, and we listened to romantic ballads sung by Daniel Santos which my mother played on the record-player. She read letters from her family in Puerto Rico and from our father. Although she loved getting his letters, his descriptions of the Roman Coliseum or the Acropolis did not interest her as much as news from *casa*—her mother and her many brothers and sisters.

Most of my mother's sentences began with *En casa* ... : at her Mama's house things were done like this and like that. At any place in the world other than her beloved *Isla* my mother would have been homesick: perpetual nostalgia, constant talk of return, that was my mother's chosen method of survival. When she looked into her looking-glass, what did she see? Another face, an old woman nagging, nagging, at her—*Don't bury me in foreign soil* ...

> *A sailor went to see, sea, sea,*
> *To see what her could see, see, see,*
> *And all that her could see, see, see,*
> *Was the bottom of the deep, blue*
> *Sea, sea, sea.*

The black girls sang this jump-rope song faster and faster in the concrete play yard of the public school, perhaps not thinking of the words, landlocked in the city, never having seen the deep, blue sea. I thought of my father when I heard it.

The deep blue sea for my father was loneliness. He had joined the U.S. military service at eighteen, the very same year he had married, because for the young men of Puerto Rico who did not have money in 1951, it was the only promise of a future away from the cane fields of the island or the factories of New York City. He had been brought up to expect better things. My father had excelled in school and was president of his senior class. In my mother, whom he met when she was just fourteen, he must have seen the opposite of himself. He had forsaken his early dreams for her love, and later for the future of his children.

His absences from home seemed to be harder on him than on us. Whatever happened to him during those years, most of it, I will never know. Each time he came home he was a quieter man. It was as if he were drowning in silence and no one could save him. His main concern was our education, and I remember showing him my school papers, which he would pore over as if he were reading a fascinating book.

He would listen attentively while Mother recounted the ordinary routine of our days to him, taking it all in like nourishment. He asked endless questions. Nothing was too trivial for his ears. It was as if he were attempting to live vicariously each day he had missed with us. And he never talked about the past; unlike our mother, he had no yearning to return to the Island that held no promise for him. But he did not deprive her of her dream of home either. And her need to be with her family may have been what prompted him to devise the complex system of back-and-forth travel that I experienced most of my childhood. Every time he went to Europe for six months, we went back with Mother to her mother's *casa*; upon his return to Brooklyn Yard, he would wire us, and we would come back. Cold/hot, English/Spanish; that was our life.

I remember my father as a man who rarely looked into mirrors. He would even comb his hair looking down. What was he afraid of seeing? Perhaps the monster over his shoulder was his lost potential. He was a sensitive, intellectual man whose energies had to be entirely devoted to survival. And that is how many minds are wasted in the travails of immigrant life.

And so, life was difficult for my parents, and that means that it was no more and no less painful than for others like them: for the struggle, *la lucha*, goes on all around for people who want to be a piece that fits in the American puzzle, to get a share in the big picture; but, of course, I see that in retrospect. At fourteen and for a few years after, my concerns were mainly focused on the alarms going off in my body warning me of pain or pleasure ahead.

I fell in love, or my hormones awakened from their

long slumber in my body, and suddenly the goal of my
days was focused on one thing: to catch a glimpse of my
secret love. And it had to remain secret, because I had,
of course, in the great tradition of tragic romance, chosen to love a boy who was totally out of my reach. He
was not Puerto Rican; he was Italian and rich. He was
also an older man. He was a senior at the high school
when I came in as a freshman. I first saw him in the
hall, leaning casually on a wall that was the border line
between girlside and boyside for underclassmen. He
looked extraordinarily like a young Marlon Brando—
down to the ironic little smile. The total of what I knew
about the boy who starred in every one of my awkward
fantasies was this: that he was the nephew of the man
who owned the supermarket on my block; that he often had parties at his parents' beautiful home in the
suburbs which I would hear about; that this family had
money (which came to our school in many ways)—and
this fact made my knees weak: and that he worked at
the store near my apartment building on weekends and
in the summer.

My mother could not understand why I became so
eager to be the one sent out on her endless errands. I
pounced on every opportunity from Friday to late Saturday afternoon to go after eggs, cigarettes, milk (I tried
to drink as much of it as possible, although I hated the
stuff)—the staple items that she would order from the
"American" store.

Week after week I wandered up and down the aisles,
taking furtive glances at the stock room in the back,
breathlessly hoping to see my prince. Not that I had
a plan. I felt like a pilgrim waiting for a glimpse of
Mecca. I did not expect him to notice me. It was sweet
agony.

One day I did see him. Dressed in a white outfit like

a surgeon: white pants and shirt, white cap, and (gross sight, but not to my love-glazed eyes) blood-smeared butcher's apron. He was helping to drag a side of beef into the freezer storage area of the store. I must have stood there like an idiot, because I remember that he did see me, he even spoke to me! I could have died. I think he said, "Excuse me," and smiled vaguely in my direction.

After that, I *willed* occasions to go to the supermarket. I watched my mother's pack of cigarettes empty ever so slowly. I wanted her to smoke them fast. I drank milk and forced it on my brother (although a second glass for him had to be bought with my share of Fig Newton cookies which we both liked, but we were restricted to one row each). I gave my cookies up for love, and watched my mother smoke her L&M's with so little enthusiasm that I thought (God, no!) that she might be cutting down on her smoking or maybe even giving up the habit. At this crucial time!

I thought I had kept my lonely romance a secret. Often I cried hot tears on my pillow for the things that kept us apart. In my mind there was no doubt that he would never notice me (and that is why I felt free to stare at him—I was invisible). He could not see me because I was a skinny Puerto Rican girl, a freshman who did not belong to any group he associated with.

At the end of the year I found out that I had not been invisible. I learned one little lesson about human nature—adulation leaves a scent, one that we are all equipped to recognize, and no matter how insignificant the source, we seek it.

In June the nuns at our school would always arrange for some cultural extravaganza. In my freshman year it was a Roman banquet. We had been studying Greek drama (as a prelude to church history—it was at a fast clip that we galloped through Sophocles and Euripedes toward the early Christian martyrs), and our young, energetic Sister Agnes was in the mood for spectacle. She ordered the entire student body (it was a small group of under 300 students) to have our mothers make us togas out of sheets. She handed out a pattern on mimeo pages fresh out of the machine. I remember the intense smell of the alcohol on the sheets of paper, and how almost everyone in the auditorium brought theirs to their noses and inhaled deeply—mimeographed handouts were the school-day buzz that the new Xerox generation of kids is missing out on. Then, as the last couple of weeks of school dragged on, the city of Paterson becoming a concrete oven, and us wilting in our uncomfortable uniforms, we labored like frantic Roman slaves to build a splendid banquet hall in our small auditorium. Sister Agnes wanted a raised dais where the host and hostess would be regally enthroned.

She had already chosen our Senator and Lady from among our ranks. The Lady was to be a beautiful new student named Sophia, a recent Polish immigrant, whose English was still practically unintelligible, but whose features, classically perfect without a trace of makeup, enthralled us. Everyone talked about her gold hair cascading past her waist, and her voice which could carry a note right up to heaven in choir. The nuns wanted her for God. They kept saying that she had vocation. We just looked at her in awe, and the boys seemed afraid of her. She just smiled and did as she was told. I don't know what she thought of it all. The main privilege of beauty is that others will do almost everything for you, including thinking.

Her partner was to be our best basketball player, a tall, red-haired senior whose family sent its many offspring to our school. Together, Sophia and her senator looked like the best combination of immigrant genes our community could produce. It did not occur to me to ask then whether anything but their physical beauty qualified them for the starring roles in our production. I had the highest average in the church history class, but I was given the part of one of many "Roman Citizens." I was to sit in front of the plastic fruit and recite a greeting in Latin along with the rest of the school when our hosts came into the hall and took their places on their throne.

On the night of our banquet, my father escorted me in my toga to the door of our school. I felt foolish in my awkwardly draped sheet (blouse and skirt required underneath). My mother had no great skill as a seamstress. The best she could do was hem a skirt or a pair of pants. That night I would have traded her for a peasant woman with a golden needle. I saw other Roman ladies emerging from their parents' cars looking authentic in sheets of material that folded over their bodies like the garments on a statue by Michaelangelo. How did they do it? How was it that I always got it just slightly wrong, and worse, I believed that other people were just too polite to mention it. "The poor little Puerto Rican girl," I could hear them thinking. But in reality, I must have been my worst critic, self-conscious as I was.

Soon, we were all sitting at our circle of tables joined together around the dais. Sophia glittered like a golden statue. Her smile was beatific: a perfect, silent Roman lady. Her "senator" looked uncomfortable, glancing around at his buddies, perhaps waiting for the ridicule that he would surely get in the locker room later. The nuns in their black habits stood in the background watching us. What were they supposed to be, the Fates? Nubian slaves? The dancing girls did their modest little dance to tinny music from their finger cymbals, then

the speeches were made. Then the grape juice "wine"
was raised in a toast to the Roman Empire we all knew
would fall within the week—before finals anyway.

All during the program I had been in a state of con-
trolled hysteria. My secret love sat across the room
from me looking supremely bored. I watched his every move, taking him in gluttonously. I relished the
shadow of his eyelashes on his ruddy cheeks, his pouty
lips smirking sarcastically at the ridiculous sight of our
little play. Once he slumped down on his chair, and
our sergeant-at-arms nun came over and tapped him
sharply on his shoulder. He drew himself up slowly,
with disdain. I loved his rebellious spirit. I believed
myself still invisible to him in my "nothing" status as
I looked upon my beloved. But toward the end of the
evening, as we stood chanting our farewells in Latin, he
looked straight across the room and into my eyes! How
did I survive the killing power of those dark pupils? I
trembled in a new way. I was not cold—I was burning!
Yet I shook from the inside out, feeling light-headed,
dizzy.

The room began to empty and I headed for the girls'
lavatory. I wanted to relish the miracle in silence. I
did not think for a minute that anything more would
follow. I was satisfied with the enormous favor of a
look from my beloved. I took my time, knowing that
my father would be waiting outside for me, impatient,
perhaps glowing in the dark in his phosphorescent white
Navy uniform. The others would ride home. I would
walk home with my father, both of us in costume. I
wanted as few witnesses as possible. When I could no
longer hear the crowds in the hallway, I emerged from
the bathroom, still under the spell of those mesmerizing
eyes.

The lights had been turned off in the hallway and

all I could see was the lighted stairwell, at the bottom of which a nun would be stationed. My father would be waiting just outside. I nearly screamed when I felt someone grab me by the waist. But my mouth was quickly covered by someone else's mouth. I was being kissed. My first kiss and I could not even tell who it was. I pulled away to see that face not two inches away from mine. It was he. He smiled down at me. Did I have a silly expression on my face? My glasses felt crooked on my nose. I was unable to move or to speak. More gently, he lifted my chin and touched his lips to mine. This time I did not forget to enjoy it. Then, like the phantom lover that he was, he walked away into the darkened corridor and disappeared.

I don't know how long I stood there. My body was changing right there in the hallway of a Catholic school. My cells were tuning up like musicians in an orchestra, and my heart was a chorus. It was an opera I was composing, and I wanted to stand very still and just listen. But, of course, I heard my father's voice talking to the nun. I was in trouble if he had had to ask about me. I hurried down the stairs making up a story on the way about feeling sick. That would explain my flushed face and it would buy me a little privacy when I got home.

The next day Father announced at the breakfast table that he was leaving on a six month tour of Europe with the Navy in a few weeks and, that at the end of the school year my mother, my brother, and I would be sent to Puerto Rico to stay for half a year at Mamá's (my mother's mother) house. I was devastated. This was the usual routine for us. We had always gone to Mamá's to stay when Father was away for long periods. But this year it was different for me. I was in love, and ... my heart knocked against my bony chest at this thought ... he loved me too? I broke into sobs and left the table.

In the next week I discovered the inexorable truth about parents. They can actually carry on with their plans right through tears, threats, and the awful spectacle of a teenager's broken heart. My father left me to my mother who impassively packed while I explained over and over that I was at a crucial time in my studies and that if I left my entire life would be ruined. All she would say was, "You are an intelligent girl, you'll catch up." Her head was filled with visions of *casa* and family reunions, long gossip sessions with her mamá and sisters. What did she care that I was losing my one chance at true love?

In the meantime I tried desperately to see him. I thought he would look for me too. But the few times I saw him in the hallway, he was always rushing away. It would be long weeks of confusion and pain before I realized that the kiss was nothing but a little trophy for his ego. He had no interest in me other than as his adorer. He was flattered by my silent worship of him, and he had *bestowed* a kiss on me to please himself, and to fan the flames. I learned a lesson about the battle of the sexes then that I have never forgotten: the object is not always to win, but most times simply to keep your opponent (synonymous at times with "the loved one") guessing.

But this is too cynical a view to sustain in the face of that overwhelming rush of emotion that is first love. And in thinking back about my own experience with it, I can be objective only to the point where I recall how sweet the anguish was, how caught up in the moment I felt, and how every nerve in my body was involved in this salute to life. Later, much later, after what seemed like an eternity of dragging the weight of unrequited love around with me, I learned to make myself visible and to relish the little battles required to win the greatest prize of all. And much later, I read and understood Camus' statement about the subject that concerns both adolescent and philosopher alike: if love were easy, life would be too simple.

The Habit of Movement

Nurtured in the lethargy of the tropics,
the nomadic life did not suit us at first.
We felt like red balloons set adrift
over the wide sky of this new land.
Little by little we lost our will to connect
and stopped collecting anything heavier to carry
than a wish.
We took what we could from books borrowed
in Greek temples, or holes in the city walls,
returning them hardly handled.

We bore the idea of home on our backs
from house to house, never staying
long enough to learn the secret ways of wood
and stone, and always the blank stare
of undraped windows behind us
like the eyes of the unmourned dead.
In time we grew rich in dispossession
and fat with experience.
As we approached but did not touch others,
our habit of movement kept us safe
like a train in motion—

nothing could touch us.

Quinceañera

Pregunta: ¿Qué debe hacer una mu-
            chacha para que los jóvenes
            anden detrás de ella?
Respuesta: Irse delante de ellos.

—A Puerto Rican Riddle

I was fifteen years old when I went to Puerto Rico
as a child for the last time. The next time I would visit
the island would be as a young bride years later. That
last summer that I was a part of my mother's matriarchal tribe I learned a few things about what it meant to
become a woman in Puerto Rico.

As a young child, my grandmother's house had
seemed a labyrinth of wonders, with its haphazard collection of rooms, few doors that locked, and the constant bustle of aunts, uncles, and cousins. At fifteen,
resentful of having once again been yanked from my
environment of Paterson, New Jersey—which I thought
I was beginning to conquer with my growing mastery
of its rules—I felt smothered by the familial press of
Mamá's house. It was a place where a demand for privacy was considered rude, where people asked where
you were going if you tried to walk out of a room, where
an adolescent girl was watched every minute by the
women who acted as if you carried some kind of time-
bomb in your body that might go off at any minute;

and, worse, they constantly warned you about your behavior around men: don't cross your legs like that when a man is in the room, don't walk around in your pajamas, never interrupt their conversations. It did not matter that the men were my uncles, my cousins, and my brother. Somehow my body with its new contours and new biological powers had changed everything: half of the world had now become a threat, or felt threatened by its potential for disaster.

The devastation caused by female bodies was evident everywhere to me that summer. One of my uncles, recently married, still lived at Mamá's with his pregnant bride who had to be treated with maddening delicacy. She demanded odd things to eat which everyone scrambled to get, lest she be crossed into a difficult childbirth. She cried for no reason, took naps in the middle of the day, and everyone tip-toed around her talking in whispers. It was obvious to me that she was having the time of her life, taking advantage of a perfectly normal pregnancy to act like an invalid. I learned from my mother when I complained to her in private, that it was the right of a woman to demand attention when expecting her first child—life would get hard enough later.

Across the street lived a less fortunate new mother. Nora was a few months older than me. I remembered her from school in past months that I had spent at Mamá's. She always seemed more mature than the other girls, and no wonder. She had a whole troop of younger brothers and sisters at home that she had to mind while her mother worked the late shift in a factory. I heard that she had dropped out of high school in her freshman year, running off with a man twice her age. He never married her, and she returned home pregnant and looking worn-out and spiritless.

I often sat on the porch at Mamá's house that summer to get away from the chaos inside, and I would see Nora emerge from her house once in a while. She usually carried her child on her hip as she swept with one hand, or as she worked on a vegetable garden. Could she have been only sixteen? Her body was bloated in an unhealthy way, her movements were slow, as if she had no energy or no will. I was repelled by her appearance and her lethargy. I felt inexplicable anger when I saw her.

Every day Mamá would rise at five to work around the house. She had done housework since she could walk, and like an automaton programmed for life, she followed a routine of labor and self-sacrifice into her old age. Despite being the dominant character in her household—every practical decision made by any of her eight children and husband had to be approved by her—she believes to this day that a woman's life is redeemed mainly by work: hands busy all the time, doing, doing, doing for others. Mamá gave herself and others little time for leisure. Only small children were exempt from duties. They were the only ones allowed to waste time—everyone else had to be busy while in her presence. This work ethic applied specially to me, since in her eyes I was a *quinceañera,* a fifteen year old trainee for the demands of womanhood and marriage.

It was not that Mamá endorsed marriage as the only choice for women; it was just all she had been brought up to expect for herself, her daughters, and now, her granddaughters. If you did not get married, you became a nun, or you entered "la vida" as a prostitute. Of course there were some professions a woman could practice—nurse, teacher—until you found a man to marry. The worse fate was to end up alone (by that she meant no more children, rather than no man) in your old age. Mamá had never been alone in her life.

Even now, as an old woman, she fills her house with great-grandchildren whenever possible. Solitude means the denial of life to her.

And so the summer of my fifteenth year in Puerto Rico I resisted learning to cook claiming to get dizzy in the heat of the kitchen. Luckily there were so many cooks available in the house that I was not missed, only scorned.

I still took pleasure in listening to the women talk about their lives, and I still relished and memorized Mamá's *cuentos*, but by then I was beginning to recognize the subtext of sexual innuendo, to detect the sarcasm, and to find the hidden clues to their true feelings of frustrations in their marriages and in their narrowly circumscribed lives as women in Puerto Rico.

That summer I was courted and serenaded in a style that has, I think, practically gone out of fashion. It was 1967 and the rest of the world seemed to be plunging headlong into the future. Still, in this pueblo the young men would fill their pockets with nickels so that when their favorite girls passed by the centrally located bodega, they could play them love songs on the juke box. Each couple knew after many repetitions which was "their song." Unescorted or in the company of her friends, the girl was informed by custom to act aloof, not to look directly at the boy who would usually stand just outside the door of the establishment. If he were shy, he would gaze intently at his beloved; if brave, he would sing along with the record, often to the vast amusement and loud comments of the other males within the store. It was an exciting ritual of courtship, both elegant and brazen, that I had no preparation for, since the Paterson version of the "piropo," the hoots, hisses, and street-poetry that Latinos subject women to, was radically different from this dramatic, romantic wooing carried on without awkwardness and surprisingly accepted by the adults as part of the burden of having teenage children.

The deal was, I finally figured out, that no direct communication was to take place between the girl and the boy unless the romance was serious; if so, the boy had to ask permission of the girl's parents to visit her, and to escort her (in groups only) to dances, etc. This rule was, of course, violated by the couples as often as possible.

I learned the do's and don'ts of the game from direct observation. Though I had few close friends in town; I did have an uncle who was only six months older than me, and an aunt, his sister, who was a senior in high school—both of them in love that year. I was used by both of them as a buffer and an excuse to see their love-objects. I remember one week when my uncle offered to teach me how to ride a bicycle. Everyone was surprised at the offer since his favorite activity was "béisbol" and he was hardly ever at home. My mother accepted the offer and one day we took off through town with me as passenger and him pedalling furiously. When we reached the countryside he stopped to catch his breath and to explain to me that we would be picking up people along the way for a picnic by the river. He instructed me that when we next stopped in front of a house, I was to go to the door and ask for Carolina. He would stay out of sight. It did not take me long to understand his plan. I was his cover. He had an assignation with his girlfriend who would not be let out of the house for a boy, but if I pretended to be her schoolmate, she might be.

It was a fun day as other couples joined us and I got a lot of attention from a black boy named Wilson, who, like me, was covering for his sister and her guy. On the way home my uncle felt duty-bound to give me a lesson on the bicycle. Unfortunately, I lost control of it at the top of a hill and plunged right into a thicket with him running behind me, yelling at me to use my brakes—in my panic I had forgotten that they were located on the handlebar. The bicycle was scratched and bent and I got bumps and bruises which I was not able to hide for long from my vigilant mother.

There were no more bicycle trips for me after that incident, but bicycles continued to play a big part in my coming of age that summer.

The boys of the pueblo used their bicycles like their North American counterparts used their sportscars. They raced them past the girls they were pursuing; they performed tricks of bravura and recklessness on them, but mostly they rode them up and down the street past the house of their chosen women in hopes of a glimpse or a cautious wave. This happened usually at dusk, after dinner, when the sweaty games of baseball were over, a man's full day behind them; after the bath had washed away the dust of the playing field and the cologne and the Brillcream had been lavishly applied.

At Mamá's house, the adults practiced patience as my young uncle and aunt and I monopolized the bathrooms and the dressers for a couple of hours. My young uncle would then mount his slightly scarred vehicle and ride off to "see his woman," who would be doing just what my young aunt and I were preparing to do: getting all dolled-up just to sit on the porch, hoping that the others would stay in the livingroom and watch the *novelas*. It was almost a sure thing that they would, since the Puerto Rican soap operas are habit-forming for both men and women. Unlike the day-time soaps of the U.S., the novelas are intense mini-series that carry a highly dramatic love story, replete with betrayals, broken-hearts, rebellious children, long-suffering mothers, and gallant fathers, to a predictable, but splendidly happy ending. They are episodic in formula: to miss a night's installment is like failing to sit at your sick child's bedside or being late for your daughter's wedding. The characters in these novelas become part of daily conversations. On some ocassions I had trouble keeping the characters Mamá spoke about with great feeling separated in my mind from relatives I barely knew.

But real love was more important than the travails of the star-crossed lovers of novelas, although the contrast between the actors' passionate encounters and lyrical dialogues, and the silent circling of our young men in their bicycles seem almost absurd in recollection. But the thrill of seeing the one you longed for appear at the end of the street could not be matched by any televised melodrama.

My aunt's *novio* was about to get serious. He too was entering his last year of high school. Soon he would be a working man. He was going to learn to drive a truck. He was taking shop at school. His plan was to get a job as a long distance driver and mechanic for an American business. Then he would ask her to marry him. They both knew this, yet they were enjoying the last days of their innocent courtship. She was radiant, and she clutched my hand tightly on the darkened porch as she saw him ride past slowly, lingering, almost stopping on his polished bike. It was erotic, this meeting of the eyes, the graceful sway of the young man on his machine. I pressed her hand back. I knew what she was feeling. Soon my two champions would be performing their acrobatic dances for me too.

Yes, I had two admirers: one black, one white, both handsome. Wilson, whom I had met on my ill-fated excursion with my uncle, had been playing songs for me at the bodega. They were usually about hopeless love, since I was an "Americanita," not only pale-skinned, but a resident of the North. I would be flying away in a few months. He played "Paloma Blanca" for me and any other song that mentioned the word "white" or had the theme of abandonment. He was a beautiful ebony-skinned *muchacho* whose charm was well-known throughout the town. He was attractive even to older women, a fact that made my mother wary. She warned me that Wilson was "too mature," *muy maduro* for his age. She did not say much more than, "Don't encourage him too much." At first, having been exposed to the hostilities between blacks and Puerto Ricans in Paterson, I thought that she might be acting out of prejudice because of his color, but soon I realized that race had nothing to do with her concern; she had just heard that Wilson was rapidly developing a reputation as a womanizer, and she was afraid that he would violate the limits of propriety if I gave him the chance.

I was almost tempted to do so, spurred on by her words of caution, but I had developed a "crush" on Angel Ramón, the other boy. He had curly hair, green eyes and a shy smile. He said nothing, played no records for me at the bodega, but with his intense gaze he commanded me to love him. I broke the rules of propriety with him at the first opportunity and that ended the idyll.

One afternoon I was alone on the porch, my aunt having gone to some affair or other with my mother and Mamá. I do not remember who else was at home, but no one was watching me. I waited until Angel Ramón had locked his eyes with mine and I took a chance. I rose from my chair and motioned him to follow me to Mamá's backyard garden. Looking startled, he maneuvered his bicycle into the drive. It was almost dark and what we were doing was very dangerous. I waited, heart pounding behind the house, against a cool cement wall. When I saw him around the corner, I led him by the hand into the shadows. I then turned my face up for a kiss. I closed my eyes and felt his breath, and the cool sweat of the hand I was still holding, but when I offered my lips for a kiss, he pulled away and was gone.

Angel Ramón disappeared from my neighborhood after my bold act. I was crushed, but could not tell anyone for fear of being punished. Even my aunt would not approve of such brazenness on my part. I prayed that Angel Ramón would not spread the story around and humiliate me. Later I realized that he could not say anything either: his manhood was at stake, he had refused a woman's favors, although it was only a kiss I had offered. The other boys would surely subject him to vicious harassment for his cowardice if they found out. I had made an awful mistake, broken the rules of the game, and frightened away my gentle admirer. How far this reckless act of mine set that boy back with women, I do not know; luckily for me, the summer was coming to a close and I could go back to cooler climes—to less passion and more logic.

Back in the city, as I dealt with the daily struggle of love and life—American style—I sometimes thought about the leisure of romance in the tropics; the sensuousness of allowing your heart to set its rhythms at its own pace; how love can be allowed to flower like a well-tended rose bush. It was a lyrical time. But I have not forgotten Nora either, or how dead her eyes looked, as if she had no vision of the future. The baby riding in her hip could now have children of her own, and Nora, if she lived past her 30th birthday, will be carrying her grandchildren. I still think about her when I think of my summer as a *quinceañera* and the many directions a woman's life can take, with the word "love" as the only marker to be seen at the crossroads.

Holly

For Tanya at eleven

Did I ever tell you
holly doesn't grow in that too hot place
where I was born, and that at your age
a grown-up kiss was forced on me
behind my grandmother's house
by a fourteen year old boy I caught
stealing her grapefruit?
Still green, he laughed, and threw them at me.
For that waste I took the blame. Both these facts
you'd find hard to believe: That Christmas
can happen without snow or bright lights,
and that a boy would want to kiss your mother.
I'd like you to be innocent of such a kiss
for a few more years, Tanya,
to have more days like the crisp, cool morning
when you picked armfuls of wild holly
at your grandmother's Georgia farm
under an iced sky, nothing to distract you
but the rustling of dry leaves
as you made your way deep into the woods.
Holly fills every container in my house.
I want to keep it green for you;
you want it dried to make wreaths—
its turning brown doesn't bother you,
you don't worry about the berries,

red as your cheeks that morning
when you gathered the branches,
that are now falling,
and as we crush them with our winter boots,
they stain the floor like blood.

Marina

Again it happened between my mother and me. Since her return to Puerto Rico after my father's death ten years before, she had gone totally "native," regressing into the comfortable traditions of her extended family and questioning all of my decisions. Each year we spoke more formally to each other, and each June, at the end of my teaching year, she would invite me to visit her on the Island—so I could see for myself how much I was missing out on.

These yearly pilgrimages to my mother's town where I had been born also, but which I had left at an early age, were for me symbolic of the clash of cultures and generations that she and I represent. But I looked forward to arriving at this lovely place, my mother's lifetime dream of home, now endangered by encroaching "progress."

Located on the west coast, our pueblo is a place of contrasts: the original town remains as a tiny core of ancient houses circling the church, which sits on a hill, the very same where the woodcutter claimed to have been saved from a charging bull by a lovely dark Lady who appeared floating over a treetop. There my mother lives, at the foot of this hill; but surrounding this postcard scene there are shopping malls, a Burger King, a cinema. And where the sugar cane fields once extended

like a green sea as far as the eye could see: condomini-
ums, cement blocks in rows, all the same shape and
color. My mother tries not to see this part of her world.
The church bells drown the noise of traffic, and when
she sits on her back porch and looks up at the old church
built by the hands of generations of men whose last
names she would not recognize, she feels safe—under
the shelter of the past.

During the twenty years she spent in "exile" in the
U.S. often alone with two children, waiting for my father, she dedicated her time and energy to creating a
"reasonable facsimile" of a Puerto Rican home, which
for my brother and me meant that we led a dual existence: speaking Spanish at home with her, acting out
our parts in her traditional play, while also daily pretending assimilation in the classroom, where in the
early sixties, there was no such thing as bilingual education. But, to be fair, we were not the only Puerto
Rican children leading a double life, and I have always
been grateful to have kept my Spanish. My trouble with
Mother comes when she and I try to define and translate
key words for both of us, words such as "woman" and
"mother." I have a daughter too, as well as a demanding profession as a teacher and writer. My mother got
married as a teenager and led a life of isolation and total devotion to her duties as mother. As a Penelope-like
wife, she was always waiting, waiting, waiting, for the
return of her sailor, for the return to her native land.

In the meantime, I grew up in the social flux of the
sixties in New Jersey, and although I was kept on a
steady diet of fantasies about life in the tropics, I liber-
ated myself from her plans for me, got a scholarship to
college, married a man who supported my need to work,
to create, to travel and to experience life as an individ-
ual. My mother rejoices at my successes, but is often

anxious at how much time I have to spend away from home, although I keep assuring her that my husband is as good a parent as I am, and a much better cook. Her concern about my familial duties is sometimes a source of friction in our relationship, the basis for most of our arguments. But, in spite of our differences, I miss her, and as June approaches, I yearn to be with her in her tiny house filled with her vibrant presence. So I pack up and go to meet my loving adversary in her corner of the rapidly disappearing "paradise" that she waited so long to go home to.

It was after a heated argument one afternoon that I sought reconciliation with my mother by asking her to go with me for a walk down the main street of the pueblo. I planned to request stories abut the town and its old people, something that we both enjoy for differ-ent reasons: she likes recalling the old days, and I have an insatiable curiosity about the history and the people of the Island which have become prominent features in my work.

We had been walking around the church when we saw a distinguished looking old man strolling hand-in-hand with a little girl. My mother touched my arm and pointed to them. I admired the pair as the old man, svelte and graceful as a ballet dancer, lifted the tiny figure dressed up in pink lace onto a stool at an outdoor cafe.

"Who is he?" I asked my mother, trying not to stare as we pretended to examine the menu taped on the win-dow.

"You have heard his story at your grandmother's house."

She took my elbow and led me to a table at the far end of the cafe. "I will tell it to you again, but first I will give you a hint about who he is: he has not always been the man he is today."

Though her "hint" was no help, I suddenly recalled the story I had heard many years earlier as told by my grandmother, who had started the tale with similar words, "People are not always what they seem to be, that is something we have all heard, but have you heard about the one who ended up being what he was but did not appear to be?" Or something like that. Mamá could turn any story—it did not have to be as strange and fascinating as this one—into an event. I told my guess to my mother.

"Yes," she nodded, "he came home to retire. You know he has lived in Nueva York since before you were born. Do you remember the story?"

As we continued our walk, my mother recounted for me her mother's dramatic tale of a famous incident that had shaken the town in Mamá's youth. I had heard it once as a child, sitting enthralled at my grandmother's knee.

In the days when Mamá was a young girl, our pueblo had not yet been touched by progress. The cult of the Black Virgin had grown strong as pilgrims traveled from all over the island to visit the shrine, and the Church preached chastity and modesty as the prime virtues for the town's daughters. Adolescent girls were not allowed to go anywhere without their mothers or *dueñas*—except to a certain river that no man was allowed to approach.

Río Rojo, the river that ran its course around the sacred mountain where the Virgin had appeared, was reserved for the maidens of the pueblo. It was nothing but a stream, really, but crystalline, and it was bordered by thick woods where the most fragrant flowers and herbs could be found. This was a female place, a pastoral setting where no true *macho* would want to be caught swimming or fishing.

Nature had decorated the spot like a boudoir—royal poincianas extended their low branches for the girls to hang their clothes, and the mossy grass grew like a plush green carpet all the way down to the smooth stepping-stones where they could sun themselves like *favoritas* in a virginal harem.

As a "grown" girl of fifteen, Mamá had led her sisters and other girls of the pueblo to bathe there on hot summer afternoons. It was a place of secret talk and rowdy play, of freedom from mothers and chaperones, a place where they could talk about boys, and where they could luxuriate in their bodies. At the río, the young women felt free to hypothesize about the secret connection between their two concerns: their changing bodies and boys.

Sex was the forbidden topic in their lives, yet these were the same girls who would be given to strangers in marriage before they were scarcely out of childhood. In a sense, they were betrayed by their own protective parents who could bring themselves to explain neither the delights, nor the consequences of sex to their beloved daughters. The prevailing practice was to get them safely married as soon after puberty as possible—because nature would take its course one way or another. Scandal was to be avoided at all costs.

At the río, the group of girls Mamá grew up with would squeal and splash away their last few precious days as children. They would also wash each other's hair while sitting like brown nyads upon the smooth rocks in the shallow water. They had the freedom to bathe nude, but some of them could not break through a lifetime of training in modesty and would keep their chemises and bloomers on. One of the shyest girls was Marina. She was everyone's pet.

Marina was a lovely young girl with her *café-con-leche* skin and green eyes. Her body was willowy and her thick black Indian hair hung down to her waist. Her voice was so soft that you had to come very close to hear what she was saying during the rare times when she did speak. Everyone treated Marina with special consideration, since she had already known much tragedy by the time she reached adolescence. It was due to the traumatic circumstances of her birth, as well as her difficult life with a reclusive mother, all the girls believed, that Marina was so withdrawn and melancholy as she ended her fifteenth year. She was surely destined for convent life, they all whispered when Marina left their company, as she often did, to go sit by herself on the bank, and to watch them with her large, wet, sad eyes.

Marina had fine hands and all the girls liked for her to braid their hair at the end of the day. They argued over the privilege of sitting between her legs while Marina ran her long fingers through their hair like a cellist playing a soothing melody. It caused much jealousy that last summer before Mamá's betrothal (which meant it was the last summer she could play at the río with her friends) when Marina chose to keep company only with Kiki, the mayor's fourteen year old daughter who had finally won permission from her strict parents to bathe with the pueblo's girls at the river.

Kiki would be a pale fish among the golden tadpoles in the water. She came from a Spanish family who believed in keeping the bloodlines pure, and she had spent all of her childhood in the cool shade of mansions and convent schools. She had come to the pueblo to prepare for her debut into society, her *quinceañera*, a fifteenth birthday party where she would be dressed like a princess and displayed before the Island's eligible bachelors as a potential bride.

Lonely for the company of girls her age, and tired of the modulated tones of afternoons on the verandah with her refined mother, Kiki had pressured her father to give her a final holiday with the other girls, whom she would see going by the mansion, singing and laughing on their way to the río. Her father began to see the wisdom of her idea when she mentioned how democratic it would seem to the girls' parents for the mayor's daughter to join them at the river. Finally, he agreed. The mother took to her bed with a sick headache when she thought of her lovely daughter removing her clothes in front of the uncouth spawn of her husband's constituents: rough farmers and their sun-darkened wives.

Kiki removed all her clothes with glee as soon as the group arrived at the river. She ran to the water tossing lace, satin, and silk over her head. She behaved like a bird whose cage door had been opened for the first time. The girls giggled at the sight of the freckles on her shoulders, her little pink nipples, like rosebuds, her golden hair. But since she was the mayor's daughter, they dared not get too close. They acted more like her attendants than her friends. Kiki would have ended up alone again if it had not been for Marina.

Marina was awestruck by the exuberant Kiki; and Kiki was drawn to the quiet girl who watched the others at play with such yearning. Soon the two girls were inseparable. Marina would take Kiki's wet hair, like molten gold, into her brown hands and weave it into two perfect plaits which she would pin to the girl's head like a crown. It was fascinating to watch how the two came together wordlessly, like partners in a *pas de deux*.

It was an idyllic time, until one afternoon Marina and Kiki did not return to the river from an excursion into the woods where they had ostensibly gone to gather flowers. Mamá and her friends searched for them until

nearly dark, but did not find them. The mayor went in
person to notify Marina's mother of the situation. What
he found was a woman who had fallen permanently into
silence: secluded in a secret place of shadows where she
wished to remain.

It was the events of one night long ago that had made
her abandon the world.

Marina's mother had lost her young husband and
delivered her child prematurely on the same night. The
news that her man had been drowned in a fishing accident had brought on an agonizing labor. She had had
a son, a tiny little boy, perfect in his parts, but sickly.
The new mother, weakened in body and mind by so
much pain, had decided that she preferred a daughter
for company. Hysterically, she had begged the anxious
midwife to keep her secret. And as soon as she was able
to walk to church, she had the child dressed in a flowing
gown of lace and had her christened Marina. Living the
life of a recluse, to which she was entitled as a widow,
and attended by her loyal nurse, and later, by her quiet
obedient Marina, the woman had slipped easily out of
reality.

By the time Marina was old enough to discover the
difference between her body and the bodies of her girl-
friends, her mother had forgotten all about having borne
a son. In fact, the poor soul would have been horrified
to discover a man under her roof. And so Marina kept
up appearances, waiting out her body's dictates year by
year. The summer that Kiki joined the bathers at the
río, Marina had made up her mind to run away from
home. She had been in torment until the blonde girl
had appeared like an angel, bringing Marina the balm
of her presence and the soothing touch of her hands.

The mayor found the woman sitting calmly in a
rocking chair. She looked like a wax figure dressed in

widow's weeds. Only her elegant hands moved as she crocheted a collar for a little girl's dress. And although she smiled deferentially at the men speaking loudly in her parlor, she remained silent. Silence was the place she had inhabited for years, and no one could draw her out now.

Furious, the mayor threatened to have her arrested. Finally it was the old nurse who confessed the whole sad tale—to the horror of the mayor and his men. She handed him an envelope with *Papá y Mamá* written on its face in Kiki's hand. In a last show of control, the mayor took the sealed letter home to read in the privacy of the family mansion where his wife was waiting, still under the impression that the two girls had been kidnapped for political reasons.

Kiki's letter explained briefly that she and *Marino* had eloped. They had fallen in love and nothing and no one could change their minds about getting married. She had sold her pearl necklace—the family heirloom given to her by her parents to wear at her *quinceañera*, and they were using the money for passage on the next steamship out of San Juan to New York.

The mayor did not finish his term in office. He and his wife, now a recluse, exiled themselves to Spain.

"And Marina and Kiki?" I had asked Mamá, eager for more details about Kiki and Marino, "What happened to them?"

"What happens to *any* married couple?" Mamá had replied, putting an end to her story. "They had several children, they worked, they got old ... " She chuckled gently at my naiveté.

* * *

On our way back through town from our walk, Mother and I again saw Marino with his pretty granddaughter. This time he was lifting her to smell a white rose that grew from a vine entangled on a tree branch. The child brought the flower carefully to her nose and smelled it. Then the old man placed the child gently back on the ground and they continued their promenade, stopping to examine anything that caught the child's eye.

"Do you think he made a good husband?" I asked my mother.

"He would know what it takes to make a woman happy," she said as she turned to face me, and winked in camaraderie.

As I watched the gentle old man and the little girl, I imagined Marina sitting alone on the banks of a river, his heart breaking with pain and wild yearnings, listening to the girls asking questions he could have answered; remaining silent; learning patience, until love would give him the right to reclaim his original body and destiny. Yet he would never forget the lessons she learned at the río—or how to handle fragile things. I looked at my mother and she smiled at me; we now had a new place to begin our search for the meaning of the word *woman*.

Common Ground

Blood tells the story of your life
in heartbeats as you live it;
bones speak in the language
of death, and flesh thins
with age when up
through your pores rises
the stuff of your origin.

These days,
when I look in the mirror I see
my grandmother's stern lips
speaking in parentheses at the corners
of my mouth of pain and deprivation
I have never known. I recognize
my father's brows arching in disdain
over the objects of my vanity, my mother's
nervous hands smoothing lines
just appearing on my skin,
like arrows pointing downward
to our common ground.

— relationship b/w mother + daughter

The Last Word

> "I did that," says my memory.
> "I did not," says my pride; and
> memory yields."

—Nietzsche, *Beyond Good and Evil*

My mother opens the photo album to a picture of my father as a very young man in an army uniform. She says to me, "You had not met your father yet when this photograph was taken. He left for Panama when I was a couple of months pregnant with you, and didn't get back until you were two years old."

I have my own "memories" about this time in my life, but I decide to ask her a few questions, anyway. It is always fascinating to me to hear her version of the past we shared, to see what shades of pastel she will choose to paint my childhood's "summer afternoon."

"How did I react to his homecoming?" I ask my mother whose eyes are already glazing over with grief and affection for her husband, my father, dead in a car wreck now for over a decade. There are few pictures of him in middle age in her album. She prefers to remember him as the golden boy she married, forever a young man in military uniform coming home laden with gifts from exotic places for us.

"You were the happiest little girl on the island, I believe." She says smiling down at his picture. "After a

162

few days of getting acquainted, you two were inseparable. He took you everywhere with him."

"Mother ... " In spite of my resolve, I am jarred by
the disparity of our recollections of this event. "Was
there a party for him when he returned? Did you roast
a pig out in the backyard. I remember a fire ... and an
accident ... involving me."

She lifts her eyes to meet mine. She looks mildly
surprised.

"You were only a baby ... what is it that you think
happened on that day?"

"I remember that I was put in a crib and left alone.
I remember many people talking, music, laughter." I
want her to finish the story. I want my mother to tell
me that what I remember is true. But she is stubborn
too. Her memories are precious to her and although she
accepts my explanations that what I write in my poems
and stories is mainly the product of my imagination,
she wants certain things she believes are true to remain
sacred, untouched by my fictions.

"And what is this accident you remember? What
do you think happened at your father's homecoming
party?" Her voice has taken on the deadly serious tone
that has always made me swallow hard. I am about to
be set straight. I decide to forge ahead. *This is just
an experiment,* I tell myself. I am comparing notes on
the past with my mother. This can be managed without
resentment. After all, we are both intelligent adults.

"I climbed out of the crib, and walked outside. I
think ... I fell into the fire."

My mother shakes her head. She is now angry, and
worse, disappointed in me. She turns the pages of the
book until she finds my birthday picture. A short while
after his return from Panama, my father is supposed
to have spent a small fortune giving me the fanciest

birthday party ever seen in our pueblo. He wanted to make up for all the good times together we had missed. My mother has told me the story dozens of times. There are many photographs documenting the event. Every time I visit a relative someone brings out an album and shows me a face I've memorized: that of a very solemn two-year-old dressed in a fancy dress sent by an aunt from New York just for the occasion, surrounded by toys and decorations, a huge, ornate cake in front of me. I am not smiling in any of these pictures.

My mother turns the album toward me. "Where were you burned?" she asks, letting a little irony sharpen the hurt in her voice. "Does that look like a child who was neglected for one moment?"

"So what really happened on that day, Mami?" I look at the two-year-old's face again. There is a celebration going on around her, but her eyes—and my memory—tell me that she is not a part of it.

"There was a little accident involving the fire that day, Hija," my mother says in a gentler voice. She is the Keeper of the Past. As the main witness of my childhood, she has the power to refute my claims.

"This is what happened. You were fascinated by a large book your father brought home from his travels. I believe it was a foreign language dictionary. We couldn't pry it away from you, though it was almost as big as you. I took my eyes off you for one moment, *un momentito, nada más, Hija,* and you somehow dragged that book to the pit where we were roasting a pig, and you threw it in."

"Do you know why I did that, Mother?" I am curious to hear her explanation. I dimly recall early mentions of a valuable book I supposedly did away with in the distant past.

"Why do children do anything they do? The fire

attracted you. Maybe you wanted attention. I don't know. But," she shakes her finger at me in mock accusation, "if you remember a burning feeling, the location of this fire was your little behind after I gave you some *pan-pan* to make sure you didn't try anything like that ever again." — likes to shur out pain + past

We both laugh at her use of the baby word for a spanking that I had not heard her say in three decades.

"That is what really happened?"

"*Es la pura verdad*," she says. "Nothing but the truth."

But that is not how *I* remember it.

Lessons of the Past

For my daughter

I was born the year my father learned to march in
      step
with other men, to hit bull's eyes, to pose for sepia
      photos
in dress uniform outside Panamanian nightspots—
      pictures
he would send home to his pregnant teenage bride
      inscribed:
To my best girl.

My birth made her a madonna, a husbandless young
      woman
with a legitimate child, envied by all the tired
      women
of the pueblo as she strolled my carriage down dirt
      roads,
both of us dressed in fine clothes bought with army
      checks.

                        When he came home,
he bore gifts: silk pajamas from the orient for her;
      a pink
iron crib for me. People filled our house to wel-
      come him.
He played Elvis loud and sang along in his new
      English.
She sat on his lap and laughed at everything.
They roasted a suckling pig out on the patio. Later,

no one could explain how I had climbed over the
    iron bars
and into the fire. Hands lifted me up quickly, but
    not before
the tongues had licked my curls.

                    There is a picture of me
taken soon after: my hair clipped close to my
    head,
my eyes enormous—about to overflow with fear.
I look like a miniature of one of those women
in Paris after World War II, hair shorn,
being paraded down the streets in shame,
for having loved the enemy.

                But then things changed,
and some nights he didn't come home. I remember
hearing her cry in the kitchen. I sat on the rocking
    chair
waiting for my cocoa, learning how to count, *uno,*
    dos, tres,
cuatro, cinco, on my toes. So that when he came in,
smelling strong and sweet as sugarcane syrup,
I could surprise my *Papasito*—
who liked his girls smart, who didn't like crybabies—

with a new lesson, learned well.

The past is often

write a story about a memory
attempting to see both sides
of the story. Write 1 paragraph
with your own account, then
take another's view in the next.
compare the two.